1,000,000 Books

are available to read at

www.ForgottenBooks.com

Read online
Download PDF
Purchase in print

ISBN 978-0-331-32429-7
PIBN 11201802

This book is a reproduction of an important historical work. Forgotten Books uses
state-of-the-art technology to digitally reconstruct the work, preserving the original format
whilst repairing imperfections present in the aged copy. In rare cases, an imperfection in
the original, such as a blemish or missing page, may be replicated in our edition. We do,
however, repair the vast majority of imperfections successfully; any imperfections that
remain are intentionally left to preserve the state of such historical works.

Forgotten Books is a registered trademark of FB &c Ltd.
Copyright © 2018 FB &c Ltd.
FB &c Ltd, Dalton House, 60 Windsor Avenue, London, SW19 2RR.
Company number 08720141. Registered in England and Wales.

For support please visit www.forgottenbooks.com

1 MONTH OF
FREE
READING

at

www.ForgottenBooks.com

By purchasing this book you are eligible for one month membership to ForgottenBooks.com, giving you unlimited access to our entire collection of over 1,000,000 titles via our web site and mobile apps.

To claim your free month visit:

www.forgottenbooks.com/free1201802

* Offer is valid for 45 days from date of purchase. Terms and conditions apply.

English
Français
Deutsche
Italiano
Español
Português

www.forgottenbooks.com

Mythology Photography **Fiction**
Fishing Christianity **Art** Cooking
Essays Buddhism Freemasonry
Medicine **Biology** Music **Ancient
Egypt** Evolution Carpentry Physics
Dance Geology **Mathematics** Fitness
Shakespeare **Folklore** Yoga Marketing
Confidence Immortality Biographies
Poetry **Psychology** Witchcraft
Electronics Chemistry History **Law**
Accounting **Philosophy** Anthropology
Alchemy Drama Quantum Mechanics
Atheism Sexual Health **Ancient History**
Entrepreneurship Languages Sport
Paleontology Needlework Islam
Metaphysics Investment Archaeology
Parenting Statistics Criminology
Motivational

CATALOGUE

OF THE

MANUSCRIPT MUSIC

IN THE

BRITISH MUSEUM.

G. WOODFALL AND SON, ANGEL COURT, SKINNER STREET, LONDON.

British museum. Dept. of manuscripts.

CATALOGUE

OF THE

MANUSCRIPT MUSIC

IN THE

BRITISH MUSEUM.

PRINTED BY ORDER OF THE TRUSTEES.

LONDON, MDCCCXLII.

ADVERTISEMENT.

In the present Catalogue is comprised a notice of the whole
of the volumes relating to Music, contained in the Depart-
ment of Manuscripts in the British Museum, up to the present period; with the exception only of such small pieces
of musical notation, intermixed with Church Services, as
were thought of not sufficient importance to be separately
described. In preparing this Catalogue for press, the Public
are chiefly indebted to the assiduity and labor of Thomas
Oliphant, Esq., Secretary of the Madrigal Society, whose
knowledge of the subject rendered his services of peculiar
value; and to insure greater accuracy, the whole of the descriptions given have been subsequently compared with the
originals, and revised by the Keeper of the Manuscripts.

F. MADDEN.

British Museum, 8th Dec. 1842.

323570

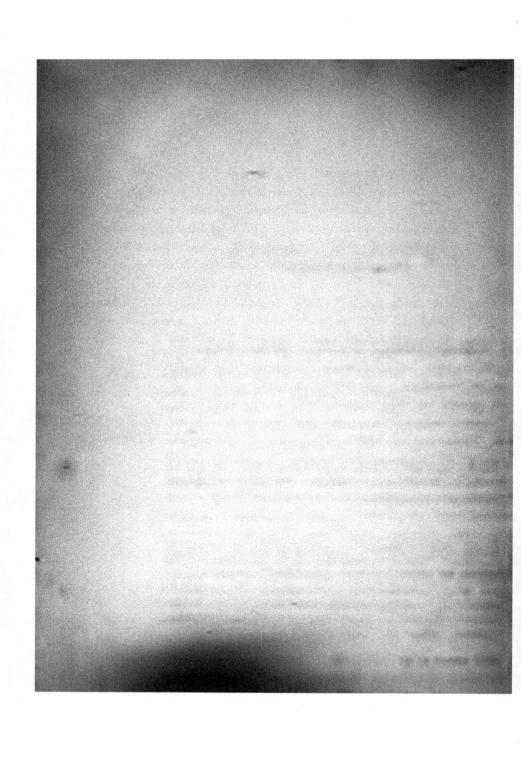

GENERAL CATALOGUE

OF

MANUSCRIPT MUSIC.

1.

" Modus intonandi Hymnos per totum annum." Beginning,
"Dominica in adventu Domini." Vellum. Duodecimo.
xvth cent. [*Royal Mss.* 2 A. ii. fol. 94.]

2.

" Regula Sancti Bernardi de modo psallendi et cantandi in
ecclesiâ." Begin. "Venerabilis sanctus Bernardus;" [See
Ms. Harl. 5235. fol. 125.] followed by a note regard-
ing the six syllables used in solmization. The volume in
which this piece is contained, was written by "Johannes
Celston," in 1466, as appears by a note at the end. Vellum.
Quarto. [*Royal Mss.* 5 A. vi. fol. 30. *b.*]

3.

The Genealogy of Christ, in Latin, adapted to musical notes.
A leaf is wanting in the middle. Vellum. Quarto. xiiith
cent. [*Royal Mss.* 7 A. iv. fol. 68.]

4.

Latin Hymns:
    To the Virgin Mary. ff. 35 and 110 *b.* xivth cent.
    For different occasions. fol. 116. xvth cent.
Vellum. Quarto. [*Royal Mss.* 7 A. vi.]

B

5.

French Songs for three voices, in separate parts: the following names of composers are given, Heyne, Bouvel, Crespieres, and Josquin [des Pres].

L'eure est venue. [Scored by Dr. Burney. See Add. Ms. 11,585.] f.21		Elle en est hors du cueur ·. fol. **39**	
Despitant fortune	22	Alez regret	40
A la mignonne de fortune	23	De vous amer follement	41
Car qui en voudroit	24	La regretée. (Heyne.)	42
Si vous voulez	25	Je n'ay dueil	43
N'ay je pas droit	26	Id.	44
En attendant	27	Car Dieu voulut	45
Il n'est vivant	28	Royne des flours	46
Vostre beaulté	29	Mon souvenir me fait morir	47
C'est mal cherce	30	L'eure que premier. (Bouvel.)	48
En effait	31	Sire, se vous ne pourvoyez. (Crespieres.)	49
Par ung jour de matinée	32	Que vous madame. (Josquin.)	50
Pour faire l'arlkymie d'amours	33	Je say tout ce qui me nuyst à savoir	51
C'est trop sur amours	34		
Soit pres ou loing	35	Je voiz partout	52
Se je vous eslongne	36	Nuit et jour sans repos	53
Helas de vous	37	Mes pensées ne me lessent	54
Ce n'est pas jeu	38	Mon cueur loyal	55

Vellum. Quarto. Latter part of the xvth cent. [*Royal Mss.* 20 A. xvi.]

6.

A book of Latin Hymns for the Festivals. Vellum. Quarto. xiith cent. [*Royal Mss.* 2 B. iv.]

7.

A tract, intitled "The Praise of Musick, the profite and delight it bringeth to Man, and other the creatures of God, and the necessarye use of it in the service and Christian Churche of God." Begin. "As it may welle be counted a needles labour." Folio. Early part of the xviith cent. [*Royal Mss.* 18 B. xix. fol. 72.]

8.

A description of the musical instruments mentioned in the Old Testament; ascribed to St. Jerome. Begin. "Tibi, Dardane, de aliis." · Vellum. Quarto. xith cent. [*Royal Mss.* 8 c. iii. fol. 1.]

Printed among the works of St. Jerome, ed. Paris, fol. 1706. tom. v. col. 191.

9.

A book of Latin Hymns, in musical notation, without lines; a beautiful manuscript. Vellum. Quarto. xith cent. [*Royal Mss.* 8 c. xiii.]

10.

Three anonymous treatises, begin.
" Est autem unisonus," fol. 50. xivth cent.
" Cum in isto tractatu de figuris." fol. 54. xivth cent.
" Cognita modulatione melorum." fol. 59. xiiith cent.
Vellum. Quarto. [*Royal Mss.* 12 c. vi.] *addit.*
    See other copies of these treatises in Ms. *Sloane* 4909.

11.

St. Augustine, his six books on Music (composed towards
the end of the fourth century). They are .printed with his
other works. Vellum. Folio. xivth cent. [*Royal Mss.* 5
n. x. fol. 30.]

12.

A volume, finely written, containing a Latin poem in honour
of King Henry VIII., beginning " Psallite felices," set
to music for four voices by —— Sampson ; also Latin
Motetts for three, four, and five voices, one of which is composed by Sampson, and another by Benedictus de Opiciis.
At the beginning is a circular enigmatical " Canon fuga in
dyatessaron," with an illuminated rose in the centre. This
volume belonged to Henry VIII. On the fly-leaf is the
following inscription, " Me fieri ac componi fecit, P. O.
1516." Vellum. Folio. [*Royal Mss.* 11 E. xi.]

13.

A finely written collection of Latin Hymns or Motetts for four
voices, originally belonging to King Henry VIII. The composers' names do not appear.
    Bound up with this volume is an enigmatical canon in a
circular form, to the words " Honi soit qui mal y pense."
Vellum. Folio. Early part of the xviith cent. [*Royal Mss.*
8 G. vii.]

14.

The Lamentations of Jeremiah, in Latin, for five voices, in separate parts. 5 vols. Quarto. xviith cent. [*Append. to
Royal Mss.* 12—16.]

15.

Motetts to Latin words, for six, eight, nine, and ten voices, collected by, or originally belonging to, Dyricke Gerarde, whose
name is on the title-page. Two of the part books are im-

perfect at the beginning. The composers' names are not
given.

N.B. The foliation refers to the *Superius* Book.

6 vols. Oblong Quarto. xvith cent. [*Append. to Royal
Mss.* 17–22.]

16.

Motetts and Songs to Latin, French, English, and Italian
words. It does not appear for how many voices they were
written; but only three parts are here given: viz., *Cantus*,
Contra Tenor, and *Tenor*.

At the end of the *Cantus* book is a fragment of what seems
to be a canon in four parts, composed by Dyricke Gerarde,
by whom probably the collection was made. The names of
the composers do not appear.

Proba me Domine	fol. 14 b.	Si bona suscepimus	fol. 27 b.
Prenes plaisir	15 b.	Dominus dedit, Dominus abstulit	28 b.
Oncques amour	16 b.	Parvulus filius hodie natus est	29 b.
Tant que en amour	17 b.	Fremuit spiritus Jhesus	30 b.
Amour au cœur (omitted in Tenor Book)	18 b.	Levavi oculos meos	31 b.
		Mon cœur chante	32
Par vous seule	19 b.	Vias tuas, Domine, demonstra	32 b.
Si j'ay du mal	20 b.	Lorde be my Judge	33 b.
En attendant	21	Ego flos campi	34 b.
Donez secours	21 b.	La neve i monti intorno	35 b.
Tous mes amis	22	Omnibus in rebus	37 b.
Ta bonne grace	22 b.	Ex animo cuncti rogitemus	38 b.
Je ne scay pas coment	23 b.	Heu michi, Domine	39 b.
Je ne desire que la mort	24 b.	Anima mea turbata est	40 b.
Adieu celle que j'ay servy	25 b.	Creator omnium	41 b.
Je suis ames	26 b.		

N.B. The foliation refers to the *Cantus* Book.

3 vols. Oblong Quarto. xviith cent. [*Append. to Royal Mss.* 23–25.]

17.

Motetts, Songs, and Madrigals to French, Latin, and Italian words, for four, five, six, and eight voices; some of which are composed by Dyricke Gerardo. In separate parts.

Die lume un tempo	fol. 1	Puer qui natus est	fol. 13 b.
Amor piangeva	1 b.	Pettite fleur	15
E la banda era molle	2 b.	Cette belle petite bouche	15 b.
Gia piansi	3	Bon jour m'amye	16
Quare fremuerunt gentes	4	J'ay veu le temps. (D. G.)	16 b.
Egrediente Domino	4 b.	J'attens secours	17 b.
Dulces exuviæ (from Virgil)	5	Adieu mon esperance. (D. G.)	18
Urbem preclaram (do.)	5 b.	Animam meam dilectam	18 b.
Multiplicati sunt	6	Illuminare Jerusalem	19 b.
Ne quando dicat inimicus. (D. Gerarde.)	6 b.	Cognovi, Domine	20
		Veniant mihi	20 b.
Timor et tremor. (D. Gerarde.)	7	Da pacem, Domine	21 b.
Il foco chio sentio	8 b.	Je l'aime bien	ib.
Hodie nobis	10	Quare tristis es	22 b.
Gloria in excelsis. (D. G.)	10 b.	Occurrerunt Maria et Martha	23
Ascendens Christus	ib.	Ad te levavi oculos	24 b.
Fidem refondens	12	Miserere nostri	25
Amy souffres	13		

N.B. The foliation refers to the *Tenor* Book.

5 vols. Oblong Quarto. xviith cent. [*Append. to Royal Mss.* 26–30.]

18.

Motetts and Songs to Latin, English, and French words, for five, six, and eight voices. A collection apparently made by Dyricke Gerarde. The composers' names are not given.

Christus factus est	fol. 2 b.	Se dire je l'osoye	fol. 6 b.
Propter quod et Deus	3 b.	Vivre ne puis	7 b.
Fortem vocemus	4 b.	Je ne scay pas coment	8 b.

N.B. The foliation refers to the *Superius* Book.

5 vols. Oblong Quarto. XVIIth cent. [*Append. to Royal Mss.* 31–35.]

19.

Alberti (Innocent). A set of Madrigals, in parts for five voices, with the following title, " Anno Domini MDLXVIII. Pro illustrissimo ac ex^mo Domino Henrico Comiti de Arundelle, Quadraginta et sex Cautiones in Italica lingua (quod vulgo vocant Madrigali) ad quinque voces, composite ab Innocentio Alberti de Tarvisio, in presentiarum Musico illustrissimi ac ex^mi Principis Domini Alphonsi, Ducis Ferrarie, et ab illo notate ac scripte, anno superscripto." On the covers are inserted oval metallic plates, silvered over, and bearing the badge of the house of Arundel, namely, a running horse, with an oak sprig in his mouth.

5 vols. Oblong Quarto. [*Append. to Royal Mss.* 36—40.]

20.

A volume of French Songs, for four voices, of the time of King Henry VIII. On the covers are stamped the royal arms. The composers' names are not given.

4 vols. Oblong Quarto. Early part of the xvith cent. [*Append. to Royal Mss.* 41—44.]

21.

Sacred music for four voices, consisting of a Kyrie eleeson, &c., for each day of the week; probably used in the royal chapel. On the covers are stamped the arms of King Henry VIII. and Catherine of Arragon. In separate parts. 4 vols. Oblong Quarto. Early part of the xvith cent. [*Append. to Royal Mss.* 45—48.]

22.

A collection of Songs and Motetts, to French and Latin words, for five, six, seven, and eight voices, made by Dyricke Gerarde, composed by himself and others, viz. Latfeur, Morel, Damianus Havericq, Noe Trnie, George Paon, Dominicus Phinot, Nicolas Gombert, Jac. Clemens, Thomas Crequillon, Nicolaus De Wismes. In separate parts.

J'attens secours de ma seulle pensée . .	Latfeur .	. . fol.	1
Bon jour, bon an, et bone vie	Morel .	. . .	2
C'est grand plaisir	Havericq	. . ib.	
Hodie nobis celorum rex ⎱			
Gloria in excelsis . . . ⎰	N. Truie	. . .	2 b.
Domine quinque talenta	G. Paon	. . .	3 b.
Ecce alia quinque.	id.	. . . .	4
Laudem dicite Deo nostro		. . . .	4 b.
Memores nostri estote		. . . .	5
Sancta Trinitas	D. Phinot	. . .	5 b.
Sancta Maria Virgo		. . . .	6 b.
Estote fortes . ⎱			
Vos amici mei. ⎰		. . . .	7 b.
Stella ista . . . . ⎱			
Apertis thesauris suis ⎰	D. Phinot	. . .	8
Gabriel Angelus . ⎱			
Erit enim magnus ⎰	Latfeur .	. . .	9
Si mon traveil	D. Havericq	. .	10
Au joly bois	N. Gombert	. .	10 b.
Changons propos	id.	. .	11
Mon petit cœur helas	id.	. .	11 b.
Comme le cherf	Jac. Clemens	. .	12
Raison le veult	N. Gombert	. .	12 b.
Retirer il me fault	T. Crequillon	. .	13
Paine et traveil	N. Gombert	. .	13 b.
Qui pouldroit dire	id.	. .	14
J'ay mis mon cœur		. .	14 b.
Jouissance vous donneray	N. Gombert	. .	15
Mille regrets	id.	. .	15 b.
Si mon traveil.	id.	. . ib.	
Je prens congie	id.	. .	16 b.
Dum transisset sabathum ⎱			
Et valde mane . . . ⎰	D. Gerarde	. . .	17
Vivre ne puis	N. De Wismes	. .	18
Magi veniunt ab oriente . ⎱⎱			
Interrogabat magos Herodes . ⎰	D. Gerarde	. . .	18 b.
Versa est in luctum . . ⎱			
Cutis mea denigrata est. ⎰	id.	. . .	19 b.
Las voules vous	id.	. .	20 b.
C'est grand plaisir	id.	. .	21
Hates vous de me faire grace	id.	. .	21 b.
Or est venu le printemps ⎱			
Car ce jour dhuy . . ⎰	id.	. .	22
Letare Jerusalem	id.	. .	23
Deus qui superbis resistis	id.	. .	23 b.

The foliation refers to the *Superius* Part Book.

6 vols.   Oblong Quarto.   xviith cent. [*Append. to Royal Mss.* 49–54.]

23.

A volume of French Airs for a single voice, roughly noted down. Some have the tablature of accompaniment for the lute.

Fault il qu' an mal que j'ay . fol. 1		L'autre jour m'en revenant. fol. 5	
O mort, l'object de ma plaisir . 1 b.		Du fond de ma pensée . . . 5 b.	
De rien ne vous sert la con-		Dès ma jeunesse 6	
stance 2		Amarilla mia bella . . . . 10 b.	
Laissez au foreste . . . . . 2 b.		Pourquoi quittois tu ces ruis-	
Dieu vous gard 3		seaux . . . . 14 b.	
Amour, j'avouray . . . . . 3 b.		Blons cheveux 15	
Vous ne nommez 4		Il s'en va l'infidelle . . . . 15 b.	
Une agreable brunette . . . 4 b.		Esprits q'un fol amour . . . 16	

Oblong Quarto. xvith cent. [*Append. to Royal Mss.* 55.]

24.

A volume containing the instrumental score part of Latin and English Songs, roughly noted down; probably by D. Gerarde. The first words only are given.

Felix namque . . . . . fol. 1 b.		Fortune unkynde . . . fol. 22	
Non expecto . . . . . . 6 b.		Et exultavit spiritus meus . . 22 b.	
Beata viscera 7		A Magnificat in each of the	
Felix namque . . . . . . 8 b.		eight ecclesiastical tones. Every	
At fol. 11 b. is this note—		tone concludes with the *Neuma*	
" Play the playne songe iij lonke "		(or series of notes sung to one	
[long].		breath at the end of the *Evove*)	
Kirie 15		forming a recapitulation of the	
Miserere . . . . . . 15 b.		melody peculiar to itself.	
Aprè de vowse . . . . . 18 b.		Myne cuckes oo . . . . . 29 b. —	
Dum vincella 19		Te eternum Patrem . . . . 30 b.	
Grace and vertue . . . . 20 b.		A litell god fayth yn all En-	
A solis ortus cardine . . . 21 b.		land . . . . 32 —	

Oblong Quarto. xvith cent. [*Append. to Royal Mss.* 56.]

25.

The *Bassus* Part Book of Latin and French Songs for six and seven voices, for the most part composed by Orlando di Lasso, Theodoricus [Dyricke] Gerarde, Damianus Havericq, Latfeur, Clemens non Papa, Caron, Nicolaus de Wismes, Christianus Hollander, and Jos. Lupi.

Jesum corona virginum . .		. fol. 1 b.
Quocunque pergis . . . } Orl. di Lassus . {		. . 2 b.
Laus, honor, virtus . . .		. . 3 b.
Urbs beata Jherusalem . .		. . 4 b.
Novam veniens e celo . . } Theod. Gerardi {		. . 5 b.
Tonsionibus pressuris . .		. . 6 b.
Gloria et honor Deo . . .		. . 7 b.
Au revenir, las, vous m'aves laisses . *id.*		9

c

Oblong Quarto. xvith cent. [*Append to Royal Mss.* 57.]

26.

A volume containing single voice parts (chiefly tenor) of English and other Songs, very curious on account of the poetry: also several instrumental pieces for the virginals, consisting of Dumpes, Pavans and Galliardes.

The only composers named are Dr. Coper, [Cooper? mentioned as an old author by Thomas Morley,] Hugh Astone, Ralf Drake, John Ambrose, and Parker, Monke of Stratforde.

Oblong Quarto. Early part of the xvith cent. [*Append. to Royal Mss.* 58.]

27.

Neapolitan " Balli " or Balletti, in four parts ; some with words ;
intitled, " Gallyardes and Neapolytans Songes."

The above have only the titles as here given. The following have the words at length.

The foliation refers to the *Cantus* Book.

4 Vols. Small Quarto. xvith cent. [*Append to Royal Mss.* 59—62.]

28.

A volume, being the *Cantus* Part only of a collection of sacred music for four and five voices, by the following composers: William Leighton, Knt., John Dowland, John Milton [the father of the poet], Robert Johnson, Thomas Ford, Edmund Hooper, Robert Kindersley, Nathaniel Giles, Jo. Coperario, John Bull, Alphonso Ferrabosco, William Bird, Robert Jones, John Wilby, John Ward, Thomas Weelkes, Orlando Gibbons, Martin Peerson, Thomas Lupo, Francis Pilkington, and Thimolphus Thopul. Small Quarto. Early part of the xviith cent. [*Append. to Royal Mss.* 63.]

This' collection was printed by Sir William Leighton, under the title of "The Teares or Lamentacions of a sorrowfull Soule." Lond. 1614. fol.

29.

Latin Hymns to musical notes. Vellum. Quarto. xɪth cent. *[Cott. Mss.* Jul. A. vɪ. fol. 17.]

30.

Fragment of a Hymn to the words " Benedicamus Domiuo." Vellum. Quarto. xvth cent. *[Cott. Mss.* Jul. A. vɪɪ. fol. 131. b.]

31.

Fragment of part of a Mass, to the words "Laudamus te." Vellum. Quarto. xvth cent. *[Cott. Mss.* Tib. A. vɪɪ. fol. 38. b.]

32.

Colored drawings of ancient Musical Instruments, with descriptions in Latin. Vellum. Small Folio. Beginning of the xɪth cent. *[Cott. Mss.* Tib. c. vɪ. fol. 16. b.]

33.

Latin Hymn " de Sancta Cruce." Begin. " Laudes Crucis attollamus." Vellum. Folio. Early part of the xɪɪɪth cent. *[Cott. Mss.* Tib. c. xɪ. fol. 156.]

34.

Latin Hymns for the principal Festivals of the Church, beautifully written and illuminated. In the first part of this volume the musical notation is without lines. Vellum. Octavo. xɪth and xɪɪth cent. *[Cott. Mss.* Cal. A. xɪv.]

35.

A Treatise by Guido Aretinus, " De Arte Musica." Begin. " Si vis scire artèm musicam." Vellum. Duodecimo. xɪɪɪth cent. *[Cott. Mss.* Nero, A. xɪɪ. fol. 174. b.]

36.

Latin Hymns for the Festivals, &c., throughout the year; imperfect. Vellum. Folio. xvth cent. *[Cott. Mss.* Nero, ᴇ. vɪɪɪ.]

37.

Specimens of early notation without lines. Begin. " Sacerdos magnus, sanctus Martinus." Vellüm. Quarto. xɪth cent. [*Cott. Mss.* Vitell. A. xɪx. ff. 88, 89.] *[handwritten annotation]*

[handwritten annotation]

38.

A Treatise by " Johannes," by some supposed to be one of the Popes of that name, as he styles himself " servus servorum Dei," and by others to be John Cotton, an Englishman. It is dedicated " Patri suo, venerabili antistiti Fulgentio." Vellum. Quarto. xɪɪth cent. [*Cott. Mss.* Vesp. A. xɪ. fol. 131.]

Printed by Gerbertus, *Scriptores Ecclesiastici de Musica,* 1784. fol. vol. ii. p. 230, under the name of John Cotton. *[handwritten annotation]*

39.

Two French Songs. *[handwritten annotation]*
Amor veint tous fors quer de felun. *[handwritten annotation]*
Au tens d'esté ke cil oisel.

Vellum. Quarto. xɪɪɪth cent. [*Cott. Mss.* Vesp. A. xvɪɪɪ. fol. 169. *b.*]

40.

[handwritten annotation] Latin Hymns; one of which has letters in addition to the antient notation over the words. Vellum. Small Quarto. *[handwritten annotation]* xth or xɪth cent. [*Cott. Mss.* Vesp. D. vɪ. fol. 77.] *[handwritten annotation]*

41.

Latin Hymn to the Virgin. Begin. " Virtute numinis non nä- tura." Vellum. Quarto. xɪɪɪth cent. [*Cott. Mss.* Titus, A. xxɪ. fol. 90. *b.*] *[handwritten annotation]*

42.

French Songs for three voices.

Jour à jour la vie	. . . . fol. 3 *b.*	Une fois avant que mourir .	fol. 4 *b.*
Qu'en puis je mais	 4	Je me recommande humblement	5 *b.*

Quarto. xvɪth cent. [*Cott. Mss.* Titus, A. xxvɪ. fol. 3. *b.*]

43.

A volume containing the following Treatises :

" Micrologus Guidonis Aretini, Monachi, in planam musi- cam." fol. 1.

Printed by Gerbertus, *Scriptores Eccles. de Musica,* vol. ii. p. 2.

" Liber secundus ejusdam, in planam musicam, quem ap- pellat trocaicum [trochaicum] ; " in verse. fol. 12 *b.*

Printed by Gerbertus, *Scriptores Eccles. de Musica*, vol. ii. p. 25, but in the Ms. is a prologue prefixed, in prose, intitled "Prologus, in quo Guido Muse ipsum alloquenti respondit," which is omitted in the printed work.

Rules by the same; "qualiter antiphonarium neumari debeat, vel notari." Begin. "Temporibus nostris super omnes homines fatui sunt cantores." fol. 17. ✗

Printed by Gerbertus, *ib.* vol. ii. p. 34.

Portion of the " Epistola Guidonis ad fratrem Martinum, discipulum suum, in qua ponit argumentum quoddam ad inveniendum novum cantum." fol. 19.

Printed by Gerbertus, *ib.* vol. ii. p. 43.

This is elsewhere intitled " Epistola Guidonis Monachi ad Michaelem, monachum Monasterii Sanctæ Mariæ in Pomposia."

See a more complete copy in *Harl. Ms.* 3199. fol. 58 *b.*

"Tercius liber ejusdam Guidonis in Musicam, sub dialogo." fol. 20 *b.*

The prologue begins, " Quicquid igitur auctoritate."

The work begins, " Quid est musica? Veraciter canendi sciencia."

This copy is made up from two manuscripts, differing greatly at the beginning, and comprehends the " Enchiridion" of Oddo, Abbot of Cluny, printed by Gerbertus, *ib.* vol. ii p. 252.

A Treatise " De tonis, per modum dyalogi, que a quibusdam intitulatur sub nomine Beati Bernardi." Begin. " Quid est tonus ? " fol. 30.

Printed by Gerbertus, *ib.* vol. ii. p. 265.

A Treatise " In Arte Musice." fol. 35.

The prologue begins, " Quoniam quidam juvenum, amici mei."

The work begins, " Fabulose loquentes dixerunt."

" Tractatus de Tonis, a Magistro Petro de Cruce, Ambianensi." Begin. " Dicturi de tonis primo videndum est." fol. 48 *b.*

" Tractatus de Tonis, a fratre Guidone, Monacho Monasterii S. Dyonisii in Francia, compilatus." fol. 54 *b.*

The prologue begins, " Gaudere sciens brevitate."

The work begins, " Ut de tonis perfectior possit haberi noticia."

Vellum. Quarto. xivth cent. [*Harl. Mss* 281.]

44.

A Latin Song in rhyme, in two part harmony. Begin. " Veri floris sub figura." Vellum. Quarto. xivth cent. [*Harl. Mss.* 524. fol. 59.]

45.

A Gradual for the whole year, in Latin. Vellum. Folio. xivth cent. [*Harl. Mss.* 622.]

46.

A Hymn in honour of Sampson. Begin. " Samson, dux fortissime." fol. 1.

Three Hymns to the Virgin Mary. fol. 3 *b*.

Example of harmony in two parts, without words. fol. 7 *b*.

Example of harmony in three parts, to Latin and French words. Begin. " Ave, gloriosa mater." fol. 8 *b*.

Hymn to the Apostles. Begin. " Felix sanctorum chorus." fol. 9 *b*.

The celebrated *Rota* or Round to the words " Sumer is icumen in," supposed to be the earliest specimen of the kind. It is for four voices in the unison, with the addition of two others, which come in at stated intervals, at the words " Sing cucu," forming a sort of burden, called " Pes." It is printed in score by Dr. Burney, *Hist. of Music*, vol. ii. p. 407, and by Sir J. Hawkins, vol. ii. p. 96. The latter has assigned to it quite an erroneous date. fol. 9 *b*.

Two Hymns in honour of the Virgin Mary. ff. 10 and 11 *b*.

A Hymn in honour of Thomas à Becket. Begin. " Ante thronum regentis." fol. 11.

Directions for singing the musical intervals. Begin. " Est tonus sic *ut*." fol. 12 *b*.

Vellum. Quarto. xiiith cent. [*Harl. Mss.* 978.]

47.

Antiphonæ, &c., " in Natali Sancti Cuthberti, Episcopi." fol. 43.

Antiphonæ, &c., " in Natali Sancti Benedicti, Abbatis." fol. 63.

Antiphonæ, &c., " in Natali Sancti Guthlaci, Confessoris." fol. 65.

The musical notation is without lines. Vellum. Large Quarto. xith cent. [*Harl. Mss.* 1117.]

48.

A collection of Songs in the handwriting of Cornelio Galli, one of the gentlemen of the Chapel Royal in the reign of Charles II.

Penoso afflitto	. . . . fol. 1	Nel giardin della speranza	fol. 34
Perche piangete	 7	Dolce colpo	. . . 38 *b*.
Anime voi che siete	. . . . 11 *b*.	Mai più stelle spietate	. . . 40 *b*.
Sileno idolo mio	. . . . . 17 *b*.	Biondi crini . .	. . . 41 *b*.
Sera alquanto addormentato	. 24	Voglio morte	. . 44 *b*.

It is presumed these Songs are by different composers, as one of them, " Voglio morte," is in Harl. Ms. No. 1273, under the name of Carlo Manelli del Violino. Oblong Quarto. Latter part of the XVIIth cent. [*Harl. Mss.* 1261.]

49.

A collection of Italian Songs or Cantatas, composed by Giacomo Carissimi, Luigi Rossi, Alessandro Stradella, Alessandro Scarlatti, Carlo Ludovici, Domenico Gabrielli, Mario Marazzoli, Tomaso Titii, Carlo Manelli, surnamed Del Violino, Giov. Battista Vulpio, Giov. Francesco Tenaglia, Henry Firmin (an Englishman), and Pietro Simone Agostini.

Oblong Quarto. Latter part of the xviith cent. [*Harl. Mss.* 1265.]

Italian　50.

A collection of Songs and Cantatas, all anonymous.

Oblong Quarto. Latter part of the xviith cent. [*Harl. Mss.* 1266.]

51.

A collection of Italian Songs.

Oblong Quarto. Latter part of the xviith cent. [*Harl. Mss.* 1267.]

52.

A collection of Italian Songs, etc., all anonymous ; but apparently belong to some opera, as the names of characters are prefixed to some of them.

Oblong Quarto. Latter part of the XVIIth cent. [*Harl.
Mss.* 1768.]

53.

A collection of Songs similar to those in the foregoing number.

Oblong Quarto. Latter part of the XVIIth cent. [*Harl.
Mss.* 1769.]

54.

A collection of Songs and Cantatas, transcribed by Bernard
Martin Berenclow, and Dr. B. M. Berenclow, his father. The
composers named are Alessandro Scarlatti, Bernardo Pasquini, L'Abbate Colonese, Giacomo Carissimi, and Henry
Purcell.

Note.—The Songs marked thus * are also in *Harl. Ms.* 1273.

Small oblong Quarto. Latter part of the XVIIth cent. [*Harl.
Mss.* 1870.]

55.

A collection of Italian Cantatas, anonymous.

Ombre, tenebre	. . . . fol. 1	Mi contento cosi	. . . . fol. 42
Resto in sen d'un antro	. . . 16	Che sento, oh Dio	 52
In erma ripa e solitario	. . . 31	Marcato havea	. . . . . 61 b.

Oblong Quarto. Latter part of the XVIIth cent. [*Harl.
Mss.* 1271.]

56.

A collection of Italian Songs and Cantatas, for the most part
anonymous, but some composed by Giacomo Carissimi, Dominico Gabrielli, Bernardo Pasquini, Allessandro Melani,
L'Abbate Colonese, Alessandro Stradella, Pietro Francesco
Tosi, Signor Ferdinando, Carlo Pietragrua, B. M. Berenclow, Alessandro Scarlatti, and Giovanni Buononcini. In the
handwriting of Bernard Martin Berenclow and Humphrey
Wanley.

Aure vaghe, aure gioconde . fol. 1	Spero da tè, mio nume	. . fol. 43
Venticelli, che tacete. (D. Ga-	Care fonti, aure soavi	. . . 43 b.
brielli.) . . . . 1 b.	Dolcissime pene	 44
Vinto hai già. (B. Pasquini.). 4 b.	Lasciami in pace. (P. F. Tosi.) 44 b.
Almeno un pensiero. (G. Ca-	Il tempo mai non perde . . . 45
rissimi.) . . . . . . 5 b.	Cara imago. (P. F. Tosi.). . 45 b.
Il tacer non fa. (A. Melani.) . 8 b.	Son vinto, mi rendo 46
Mi contento d'un sorriso . . 10 b.	A rallegrar il mondo. (P. F. Tosi.) 46 b.
Son amante ne trovo pietà . . 12 b.	Si no à quando. . . . . . 48 b.
Aure ò voi ch'in fiato . . . 13 b.	Hò un alma. 49
Sovra il sen. (G. Carissimi.) . 14	Con le stille del mio pianto . . 49 b.
Ch'io manchi mai di fede . . 15 b.	Deggio, ò Dio, lasciar morire . 50
Fidarsi d'Irene . . . . . 17 b.	A voi torno. . . . . . . 50 b.
Su quel labro . . . 19 b. and 48	Sperar ch'il Dio d'amor . . 51
Temer di chi s'adora . . . . 20 b.	Care luci, saettatemi . . . . 51 b.
Il tempo mai non perde . . . 21 b.	La speranza in chi ben ama . 52
S'a morir voi mi guidate . . 22 b.	Son pur care al sen . . . . 52 b.
Si v'intendo, ò miei pensieri . 23 b.	Di morir già non paventa . . 53
O lumi, piangete . . . . . 24 b.	Che vuol dal mio core . . . . 53 b.
Volete così miei nemiche . . 25 b.	L'aure, le frondi 54
Io provo nel alma. (Abb. Colo-	Dal oriente chiaro. . . . . 54 b.
nese.) . . . . 26 b.	Dove son l'erbete 55
So che mi piace . . . . . 27 b.	Vaga mia con chi t'adora . . 55 b.
Se t'ama Filli. (A. Stradella.) . 28 b.	È tiranico l'impero. (D. Gabrielli.) ib.
(See *Add. Ms.* 11,588.)	Và lettando in questo petto . . 56
Deh svegliatevi occhi belli . . 29 b.	Vendetta ò cor. 57
Con man di Gelsomini . . 33 b.	Solitari passeggi. (P. F. Tosi.). 58
Lusinghiere pupille . . . . 37 b.	Ah crudela, chi ti pose . . . 59
Sisto vago, siete bello . . 38 b.	Sopra il mar del incostanza. . 59 b.
Pensieri armatevi 39	Care larve. (D. Gabrielli.) . 60
Dona mi pace . . . . . 39 b.	Vezzose pupille. (P. F. Tosi or
Piu cara del core 40	Buononcini.) . . . . . 60 b.
Pra gl'assalti di Cupido . . . 40 b.	Tù mi tenti 61
Quel bello, quel labro . . . 41	Comincia tormentarmi. Scritta
Stelle amiche 42	come le canta. (P. F. Tosi.) 62
Quanto è dolce quel velen . 42 b.	Per me funeste faci . . . . 62 b.

Oblong Quarto. Latter part of the xviith cent. [*Harl.
Mss.* 1772.]

57.

A collection of Italian Songs and Duetts, some with instru-
mental symphonies, transcribed by Humphrey Wanley, and
chiefly composed by Signor Ferdinando, Alessandro Melani,
Domenico Gabrielli, L'Abbate Colonese, Bernardo Pasquini,
Carlo Manelli, surnamed Del Violino, B. M. Berenclow, Gio-
vanni Buononcini, Alessandro Scarlatti, Vincenzo Albrici,
Aldovrandi, Marc. Antonio Ziani, Rosa Hiacinta Badalli,
Carlo Pietragrua, Alessandro Stradella, Paolo Lorenzani,
Luigi Rossi.

Note.—The Songs marked thus * are also in *Harl. Ms.* 1270.

Oblong Quarto. Latter part of the xviith cent. [*Harl. Mss.* 1873.]

58.

Two Latin Hymns to the Virgin Mary. fol. 195 b.
A Hymn to the words " Recordare domine; " from the 5th Chapter of the Lamentations of Jeremiah. fol. 426 b.
    Vellum. Small Quarto. Early part of the xivth cent. [*Harl. Mss.* 1280.]

59.

A collection of Italian Songs, Duets, and Trios by the follow-ing composers,—Luigi Rossi, Pietro Reggio, Giacomo Carissimi, Casati, Marc. Ant. Cesti, Barbara Strozzi, Francesco Cavalli, Francesco Lucio, Bonifacio Graziani, Padre Tiani, Vincenzo Albrici. At the end of the volume is this nóte: " Scritto à richesta di Mons. Didier, in Londra, anno Domini 1681. Pietro Reggio." P. Reggio was a celebrated singing master and lutist in the time of Charles II.

Vorrei sooprirti un di. Duett. (L. Rossi.) . . . . . fol. 1	Son spezzate le catene. (F. Cavalli.) . . . . . . fol. 35 b.
Tu sarai sempre. Duett. (id.) 3	Chi mi credeva instabile. (L. Rossi.) . . . . 36 b.
Pene che volete. (id.) . . . 5	Voraggini ondose . . . . . 38 b.
O misera Dorinda. Duett. (P. Reggio.) 6	Quand'hebbi d'oro il crin. (P. Reggio.) 39
(From Il Pastor fido. See another copy, Harl. Ms. 1863.)	Nò nò, mio core. (G. Carissimi.) 40 b.
Spiega un volo. Duett. (L. Rossi.) 9	Non è stabile la fortuna . . . . 42 b.
Tu giuri che è mio. Duett. (id.) 10 b.	Solitudine amena 44
Difenditi, ò core. (id.) . . . 12	Maledetta la corte. (F. Lucio.) 46 b.
Chi d'amor divien seguace . . 13	Audite sancti. Trio. (G. Carissimi.) 48
Scusatemi, non posso. . . . 14	
Ohime, madre, aita. (L. Rossi.) 15 b.	O bone Jesu. (Sig. Cassati.) . 52
Sospire, ch' uscite. (G. Carissimi.) . . . . 16 b.	Gaudia Pastores. (B. Gratiani.) 54 b.
Sta in tono mio core . . . . 17 b.	Il tempio più non è. (Padre Tiani.) . . . . 57 b.
Faville d'amore . . . . . 18 b.	Che mi giova. (Air from an opera.) 58
Egionto un corriero· 19	
V'intendo occhi. (G. Carissimi.) 21	Amor sio mi querelo. (L. Rossi.) 58 b.
Sensi voi. (M. A. Cesti.) . . 23 b.	Vo cercando la speranza. (V. Albrici.) 59
Tu mancavi à tormentarmi . . 25 b.	Sassi ch'hor quà. (P. Reggio.) 61
Tradimento amore . . . . 26 b.	Poesia del Cavaglier Marini.
T'en pentirai. (P. Reggio.) . 29	Si mi dicesti. (Trio.) . . . 63 b.
Luci belle. (L. Rossi.) . . . 31	Manda i nobili allori. (V. Albrici.) . . . . 66 b.
Rissolvetevi pensieri. (Barb. Strozzi.) . . . . 31 b.	Amor chi te die l'ali. (P. Reggio.) 67 b.
Mio ben teco il tormento. (L. Rossi.) 33	(Tirata da L'Egisto.)
All ombra d'una speranza. (id.) 34	Dite, ò cieli. Duett. (L. Rossi.) 69
Nò mio cor, non ti diffendere . 34 b.	Non più vilta. (id.) . . . . 69 b.

Folio. [*Harl. Mss.* 1501.]

60.

The Services of the Greek Church, with the musical notation. Octavo *14* xiith or xiiith cent. [*Harl. Mss.* 1613.]

    This volume is most elaborately described by Humphrey Wanley, in the Catalogue of the Harleian Manuscripts. *See Vol 2.*

61.

A Latin Hymn in honour of Saint Catherine. Begin. " Kyrie lux charitatis."

Vellum. Quarto. Early part of the xivth cent. [*Harl. Mss.* 1688. fol. 108.]

62.

The *Medius* Voice Part of a collection of Latin Hymns or Anthems by English composers of the early part of the sixteenth century. The names of the following are given: Thomas Ashwelle, Ludforde, Thomas Hyllary, Pygott, Rich. Davy, William Cornyshe, and Robert Fairfax.

Quarto. Early part of the xvith cent. [*Harl. Mss.* 1709.]

In the Catalogue of the Harleian Mss. this book is stated " to have formerly belonged (as it should seem) to the Chapel of King Henry VIII." There may have been proof of this on the original binding, but nothing now exists to warrant such an inference.

63.

" Intermedio à cinque, con Instromenti; Musica del Signor Alessandro Melani, parole del Signor Pietro Cenciani." Oblong Quarto. Latter part of the xviith cent. [*Harl. Mss.* 1792.]

This book was bought of Humphrey Wanley, who states that " the musick is finely composed, Melani having been a great master in his time."

64.

A collection of Italian Songs and Duetts (with two Latin Motetts) chiefly composed by Luigi Rossi, Pietro Reggio, Giov. Oppigniani, Marc. Ant. Cesti, Carlo Ambrosio Lunati, Paolo Lorenzano, Giov. Bat. Draghi, (Music Master to Queen Anne,) Signr. T. M. R., Giov. Francesco Tenaglia, Francesco Cavalli, Giacomo Carissimi, Alessandro Melani, and Bonifazio Graziani. Almost wholly transcribed by B. M. Berenclow.

Se dardo pungente. Duett . p. 45
Cosi si tratta, oh Dio. (G. Op-
pigniani.) 50
O quanto è dolce. (id.). . . 53
Del famoso oriente. (M. A. Cesti.) 59
Sospiri, ola, che fate 62*
Vieni pur mia libertà. . . . 68*
Sassi che hor. (P. Reggio.) . 75
Nel adirato seno. (C. A. Lunati.) 82
Hor che del ciel. (P. Reggio.) 92
Occhi belli 101
Un genio fatale mi sforza . 104
Quanto poco durate. (P. Lau-
renzano.) 107
Lasciatemi speranze 114
Sotto vedovo cielo. (M.A.Cesti.) 119
Aspettate adesso canto. (id.) . 127
Perche piangete, amanti. . . 145
Tu m'aspetasti. (M. A. Cesti.) 149
Quando amor mi darai pace . 155
Qual spaventosa tromba. (G.
B. Draghi.) 157
Non dorme mio cuore . . . 165
Più tacer non si può . . . 168
Alpi nevose e dure 175

Datti pace, O Fileno . . . p. 181
Gite pur per l'aria. (C. A. Lu-
nati.) 187
Vedi Filli gentil. (T. M. R.) . 191
Son disperato. Duett. (G. F.
Tenaglia.) 201
Da l'antro magicho. (F. Cavalli.) 206
Che faro, m'inamoro. (L. Rossi.) 215
Sera alquanto addormentato . 219
Piange, Filli. (G. Carissimi.) 234
Che mi giova 246
Fin all' ultimo respiro . . . 249
E tu resti, mia vita 254
Fileno, idolo mio. (A. Melani.) 262
Guarda ben, mio cor. Duett . 269
Cieco Dio. Duett 275
Nel adirato seno 281
Anime voi chi sete 291
Pieta spietati lumi. Duett. (L.
Rossi.) 298

Reversing the volume, are the two
following Motetts.

Læta dies, cara lux. Duett . 1
Vidi Luciferum. (B. Gratiani.) 24

Oblong Quarto. Latter part of the xviith cent. [*Harl. Mss.* 1863.]

65.

Minute Book of " The Corporacion for regulateing the Art and Science of Musique," from the 22nd October, 1661, to the 2nd July, 1679 ; containing the autographs of many of the gentlemen of the Chapel Royal during that period. Folio. [*Harl. Mss.* 1911.]

66.

" Ymnus in dedicatione Sancti Michahelis." Begin. " Christe, sanctorum decus angelorum." fol. 17 *b.*
The first and second books of Boethius " de Musica." fol. 55.
Printed amongst his Works, Basil. fol. 1570.
Vellum. Folio. xth or xiith cent. [*Harl. Mss.* 2688.]

67.

A Latin Psalter, with Hymns, Antiphonies, etc. A fine manu-script. Vellum. Small Folio. xiiith cent. [*Harl. Mss.* 2888.]

68.

A fine Lectionary, towards the end of which are several Latin Hymns in old musical notation without lines. Vellum. Small Folio. xith cent. or earlier. [*Harl. Mss.* 2889.]

E

69.

A Lectionary, in Latin, originally belonging to the Monastery of Moissac, in the province of Quercy; the responses of which are finely written in old musical notation without lines. Vellum. Small Folio. xiith cent. [*Harl. Mss.* 2914.]

70.

A Processional, in Latin, containing Hymns, Antiphonies, etc., according to the use of Salisbury. Vellum. Octavo. xvth cent. [*Harl. Mss.* 2942.]

71.

A Processional, in Latin, according to the use of Salisbury. Imperfect at the beginning and end. Vellum. Small Quarto. xvth cent. [*Harl. Mss.* 2945.]

72.

Latin Hymns, according to the use of Salisbury. Vellum. Octavo. xvth cent. [*Harl. Mss.* 2951.]

73.

Latin Hymns for the whole year. The notation without lines. Vellum. Small Quarto. xiith cent. [*Harl. Mss.* 2961.]

74.

" Ordo processionis generalis perpetuo faciendæ singulis annis die octavo mensis Maij, pro liberatione civitatis Aurelianensis." The music throughout is beautifully written. Vellum. Small Quarto, written A.D. 1642. [*Harl. Mss.* 2981.]

75.

A Latin Hymn to the Virgin. Begin. " Clemens et benigna." At the beginning is written, " Liber Sancte Marie Novi Monasterii." Vellum. Quarto. End of the xiith cent. [*Harl. Mss.* 3013. fol. 1.]

76.

Specimen of early musical notation, written at the commencement of Pope Gregory's Libri Moralium in Job. Begin. " Beate martyr, prospera." Vellum. Folio. xiith cent. [*Harl. Mss.* 3033. fol. 1.]

77.

Two Books of Airs for the Mean and Bass Viol, some of which are composed by John Bannister, leader of the King's Band [A.D. 1670]. The music is very imperfect, and probably other instrumental parts are wanting. Oblong Quarto. Latter part of the xviith cent. [*Harl. Mss.* 3187, 8.]

78.

" De constitutionibus in musica," in verse. Begin. " Constitutionum formas breviter aperiam." fol. 55 *b*.

It is a portion of the " Regulæ rhythmicæ " of Guido Aretinus. See Gerbertus, vol. ii. p. 31.

Rules by Guido Aretinus " de ignoto cantu." Begin. " Temporibus nostris super omnes homines fatui sunt cantores." (Comp. *Harl. Ms.* 281.) fol. 56 *b*.

Printed by Gerbertus, vol. ii. p. 34.

Epistle of Guido Aretinus " de ignoto cantu," omitting the prefatory matter. Begin. " Ad inveniendum igitur ignotum cantum." fol. 58 *b*.

" Quid sit Armonia." Begin. " Armonia est diversarum vocum apta coadunatio. fol. 64 *b*.

A Treatise " de Tonis." Begin. " Tonus dualem significationem habet." fol. 73.

Fifteen chapters from the Micrologus of Guido Aretinus, with the Prologue. fol. 78.

For more complete copies, see *Harl. Ms.* 281, *Sloane Ms.* 4915, *Add. Ms.* 10,335, and *Arund. Ms.* 389. It is printed by Gerbertus, vol. ii. p. 2.

Vellum. Duodecimo. xiiith cent. [*Harl. Mss.* 3199.]

79.

" Claudii Ptolemei Harmonicorum libri tres, interprete Nicolao Leoniceno." This volume is in the autograph of Franc. Gafurius, the celebrated theoretical writer, whose arms are emblazoned at the commencement. Vellum. Small Folio. Dated A.D. 1409. [*Harl. Mss.* 3306.]

80.

Portions of the work of Boethius " de Musica," namely of lib. i. capp. 13–16, lib. ii. capp. 19–28. Vellum. Folio. xth cent. [*Harl. Mss.* 3595. ff. 50–56.]

81.

A book of Latin Hymns. Imperfect at the commencement. Vellum. Folio. xvth cent. [*Harl. Mss.* 3965.]

82.

A book containing the words of Anthems by English composers, from the time of King Henry VIII. till towards the
end of the 17th century. Small Quarto. Latter part of the
xviith cent. [*Harl. Mss.* 4142.]

83.

" Musical observations and experiments in musical sounds belonging to the theorie part of music." fol. 1.
" The most exact way for the tuning of an organ, harpsechord,
virginal, or espineta." fol. 65.
" A short introduction to the knowledge of descant or com-
posing of music." fol. 69.
Quarto. Early part of the xviiith cent. [*Harl. Mss.* 4160.]

84.

The Miracles of the Virgin Mary, in French verse. Near the
beginning and in the middle of the volume some parts are
set to music. Imperfect at the end. Vellum. Folio. xiiith
cent. [*Harl. Mss.* 4401.]

85.

A volume marked at the beginning, " Humfredus Wanley e
Coll. Univ. Oxon. Dec. 24, 1697," containing
The first flute part of sundry sonatas, duetts, and trios, by
Raffael Cortevil, A.D. 1686 ; Mr. Keene, Godfrey Finger,
Mr. Morgan, Robert King, and Godfrey Keller. p. 1.
Part of a Mass for four voices, with accompaniments, by
Giacomo Carissimi. p. 73.
Part of an " Officium B. V. Mariæ musicis aptatum con-
centibus a Joanne Baptista Bassano." p. 113.
Folio. Latter part of the xviith cent. [*Harl. Mss.* 4899.]

86.

" Modus cantandi, secundum [Sanctum] Bernardum." Begin.
" Venerabilis pater Sanctus Bernardus." Vellum. Quarto.
xiiith cent. [*Harl. Mss.* 5135. fol. 123.]
See a later copy in Ms. Reg. 5 A. VI. fol. 30 *b*.

87.

Boethius de Musica. From the 23rd chapter of the first book,
to the first chapter of the fifth book. Vellum. Quarto.
xiiith cent. [*Harl. Mss.* 5237.]

88.

A collection of French Songs for two and three voices, all anonymous, except one composed by Anth. de Fevin.

Vrai dieu d'amours . . . fol. 2	Veulx Caron ne scauroit sepa-
Pour Francoyse, que plus ne voy 3	rer . . . . fol. 24
Seigneurs, que Dieu vous gard . 4	Helas, j'en suis marri . . . 25
Et pour vous faire entendre . 5	Il n'y a ici celuy 27
Je le l'airray. (A. de Fevin.) . 6	Petite fleur cointe et jolie . . 28
Mauldits soient ces mariz . . 8	A vous non autre 29
Non mudera ma constance (im-	Adieu m'amour et mon desir . 31
perfect) 10	Royne des flours 33
Pensez de faire garnison . . 12	Royne des flours 34
Si j'eusse Marion 13	Royne des flours 35
Tres doulce dame 14	L'amour de moy si est enclose . 37
Le bon espoir 16	Il fait bon aimer l'oyssellet . . 39
Souvent je mesbatz 18	Non mudera ma constance . . 41
Celle qui m'a demandé argent . 19	On a mal dit de mon amy . . 42
Dieu la gard la bergerotte . . 20	Mais que ce fust le plaisir . . 44
Adieu solas 21	Dieu gard celle de deshonneur . 46
Si j'ay perdu par mesdisans . . 22	Vrai Dieu qui me confortera . 48
Si j'aime mon amy (imperfect). 22 b.	Several of the illuminated
En despit des faulx mesdisans . 23	initial letters have been cut out.

Vellum. Quarto. xvith cent. [*Harl. Mss.* 5242.]

89.

" S. Aurelii Augustini de Musica Libri vi." At the end is the
following inscription, " Joannes Arretinus absolvit Venetiis,
1423." Vellum. Octavo. [*Harl. Mss.* 5248. fol. 1.]

90.

A book of Latin Hymns, at one time belonging to Lichfield
Cathedral. Imperfect at the beginning. Vellum. Quarto.
xvth cent. [*Harl. Mss.* 5249.]

91.

A book of Latin Hymns, etc., neatly written, but imperfect at
the beginning and the end. Vellum. Folio. Early part of
the xivth cent. [*Harl. Mss.* 5284.]

92.

A Greek Treatise on Music, in three books, by Manuel Bryen-
nius, who is supposed to have lived in the fourth century.
It has been published, together with a Latin translation, by
Dr. Wallis, Oxford, 1699.

A Greek Treatise on Music, in three books, by Aristides Quin-
tilianus, a writer of the second century. It has been published, with a Latin translation, by Meibomius, Amsterdam,
1652. Folio. xvth cent. [*Harl. Mss.* 5691.]

93.

A book of the words of English Anthems, from the time of King Henry VIII. till towards the end of 'the seventeenth century. Folio. Latter part of the xviith cent. [*Harl. Mss.* 6346.]

94.

Musical notes for the Trumpet, representing the cavalry signals *la charge, la chamade, bouteselle, à cheval,* etc.; also the notes for the horn in hunting. Quarto. Early part of the xviith cent. [*Harl. Mss.* 6461. fol. 58 *b.*]

95.

Libellus Musicalis de ritu canendi vetustissimo et novo; " comprised in three books. Begin. "Omnium quidem artium etsi varia sit introductio." Quarto. xvth cent. [*Harl. Mss.* 6525.]

96.

A Madrigal for four voices, intitled " King James his quier," composed by Henry Peacham, and written by him at the end of a book of emblems dedicated to James I. It is thus described in the Harleian Catalogue : " Cantio votiva seu congratulatoria ad Regem, in quatuor partibus, ab alumnis quatuor regnorum, Anglo, sc. Scoto, Gallo, et Hiberno con- cinenda ; ab ipso autore composita." Folio. Beginning of the xviith cent. [*Harl. Mss.* 6855. fol. 160 *b.*]

97.

The Psalm " Venite exultemus " in each of the eight ecclesi- astical tones. Imperfect at the commencement. This ma- nuscript was written in Spain, with very large notes, and is beautifully executed. Vellum. Large Folio. xvith cent. [*Harl. Mss.* 7196.]

98.

" A collection of the most celebrated Services and Anthems used in the Church of England, from the Reformation to the Restauration of K. Charles II. [continued to the end of the reign of Queen Anne], composed by the best masters, and collected by Thomas Tudway, D.M., Musick Professor to the University of Cambridge."

The six volumes containing this collection were transcribed by Dr. Tudway for Edward, Lord Harley, to whom they are

severally dedicated, in the years 1715–1720. At the end of
each volume is a table of contents, but throughout there are
many inaccuracies as to names and dates. The following is
an alphabetical list of the composers, with references to the
volumes in which their works are to be found.

ALDRICH (HENRY).

Adaptations to English words of the sixteen following Motetts of
Palestrina, Carissimi, Stradella, etc. . . . . Vol. II.

We have heard with our ears. (Palestrina.)
Why art thou so vexed.
My heart is fixed.
The eye of the Lord.
O God, the King of Glory.
Hold not thy tongue.
Give ear, O God.
Behold, now praise the Lord.
Hide not thou thy face.
I look for the Lord.
O Lord, rebuke me not. See WHITE (MATTHEW), Vol.
        III. in this collection.
O how amiable are thy dwellings.
For Sion's sake I will not hold my peace.
O pray for the peace of Jerusalem.
I am well pleased.
Haste thee, O Lord my God.

The Morning and Evening Service in G . . . . III.
Anthem. Out of the deep have I called . . . . ib.
——— O praise the Lord . . . . ib.
——— Sing unto the Lord, O ye saints . . . . ib.
——— O Lord, grant the King a long life . . . . . . ib.
The Evening Service in F . . . . ib.
Anthem. Comfort ye my people . . . . ib.
——— Who is this that cometh from Edom . . . . . . ib.
——— O Lord, our Governor . . . . ib.
——— O God, thou art my God . . . . ib.
——— Have mercy upon me, O Lord . . . . ib.
The Morning and Evening Service in A major . . . . IV.
Anthem. I will love thee, O Lord . . . . ib.
——— The Lord is King . . . . ib.
——— Give the king thy judgments . . . . ib.
——— If the Lord himself . . . . ib.
——— O Lord, I have heard thy voice . . . . ib.

AMNER (JOHN).

The Morning and Evening Service in D minor (commonly called
Cæsar's in D) . . . . I.
Anthem. O come hither and hearken . . . . ib.
——— Christ rising again . . . . ib.
The whole Service in G (commonly called Cæsar's) . . . . . III.
The whole Service in D minor . . . . IV.
Anthem. O sing unto the Lord . . . . ib.
——— Lord, I am not high minded . . . . ib.
——— Remember not, Lord . . . . ib.
——— Sing, O Heavens . . . . ib.

BARCROFT (THOMAS).

The Morning Service in G . . . . I.
Anthem. O almighty God . . . . IV.

(No 98)

BATTEN (ADRIAN).
Anthem. Hear my prayer, O God . . . . Vol. I.

BEVIN (ELWAY). The whole Service in D . . . . III.

BISHOP (JOHN).
The Morning Service in D major . . . . V.
Anthem. O Lord our Governor . . . . *ib.*

BLOW (JOHN).
The Evening Service in E minor . . . ` . . . . II.
Anthem. O Lord, I have sinned (for the funeral of Gen. Monk) . *ib.*
——— I said in the cutting off of my days . . . . . . *ib.*
——— The Lord is my shepherd . . . . *ib.*
The Morning and Evening Service in G . . . . III.
Anthem. Save me, O God . . . . *ib.*
——— O Lord God of my salvation . . . . *ib.*
——— O God, my heart is ready . . . . *ib.*
——— And I heard a great voice . . . . *ib.*
——— The kings of Tharsis . . . . ; . . . . . . *ib.*
——— Praise the Lord, O my soul . . . . *ib.*
I will alway give thanks. (The Club Anthem.) . . . . . *ib.*
The whole Service in A major . . . . IV.
Anthem. I beheld, and lo, a great multitude . . . . . . *ib.*
——— O sing unto God . . . . *ib.*
——— Why do the heathen . . . . *ib.*
——— We will rejoice . . . . *ib.*
——— O Lord, thou hast searched me out . . . . . . *ib.*
——— Thy righteousness, O God . . . . *ib.*
——— God is our hope and strength . . . . , . *ib.*
——— O God, wherefore art thou absent . . . . *ib.*

BOWMAN (JOHN). Anthem. Show yourselves joyful . . . . . V.

BRODERIP (WILLIAM).
The Morning and Evening service in D major . . . . VI.
Anthem. God is our hope and strength . . . . *ib.*

BRYAN or BRYNE (ALBERTUS). The whole Service in G . . . . II.

BULL (JOHN).
Anthem. Almighty God, who by the leading of a star . . . . I.

BYRD (WILLIAM).
The whole Service in D minor for four voices. (Printed by Boyce
for four, five, and six voices.) . . . . *ib.*
Anthem. Sing joyfully unto God our strength . . . . . . *ib.*
——— O Lord, turn thy wrath, (Ne irascaris.) . . . . . *ib.*
——— Bow thine ear. 2d Part. (Civitas sancti tui.) . . . *ib.*
——— O Lord, make thy servant . . . . *ib.*
——— Save me, O God . . . . *ib.*
——— Prevent us, O Lord . . . . *ib.*
Canon. Non nobis Domine . . . . *ib.*
    This Canon is, by tradition, ascribed to Byrd, but it appears
nowhere in print under his name during the sixteenth or seven-
teenth centuries.

CARISSIMI (GIACOMO). See ALDRICH (H.).
Compositions adapted to English words, by H. A. . . . . . . II.

CHILD (WILLIAM).
The whole Service in D major . . . . *ib.*
The Morning and Evening Service in F . . . . *ib.*
The Evening Service in A . . . ` . . . . *ib.*
The Evening Service in C minor (transposed a note higher) . . . *ib.*

(N° 98)

(No 98)

(Nvo 98)

MOLLE (HENRY).
The Evening Service in D . . . . Vol. I.
The Evening Service in F . . . . *ib.*

MORLEY (THOMAS).
The Evening Service in D . . . . *ib.*
Anthem. I am the resurrection . . . . *ib.*
———– Man that is born of woman . . . . . . *ib.*
———– I heard a voice from heaven . . . . *ib.*

MUDD (—). Anthem. God, which hast prepared . . . . **IV.**

MUNDY (WILLIAM).
Anthem. O Lord, I bow the knees of my heart. (The prayer of
Manasses.) . . . . *I.*

NALSON (VALENTINE).
The Evening Service in G . . . . **V.**
The Morning Service in G . . . . **VI.**

NORRIS (WILLIAM).
The Morning Service in G minor . . . . **IV.**
Anthem. Blessed are they that are undefiled . . . . . . *ib.*
———– I will give thanks . . . . *ib.*

PALESTRINA (PIER LUIGI DA).
Anthem. We have heard with our ears. (One of the Motetts
by Palestrina, Stradella, &c., adapted to English words by Dr.
Aldrich.) . . . . **II.**

PARSONS (ROBERT). Anthem. Deliver me from mine enemies . . **III.**

PATRICK (NATHAN). The whole Service in G minor . . . . . **I.**

PORTMAN (WILLIAM). The whole Service in G major . . . . . *ib.*

PURCELL (HENRY).
Anthem. My beloved spake . . . . **II.**
———– They that go down to the sea . . . . *ib.*
———– My song shall be alway . . . . *ib.*
The Morning and Evening Service in B flat . . . . **III.**
Anthem. Rejoice in the Lord alway . . . . *ib.*
———– Praise the Lord, O my soul . . . . *ib.*
———– I was glad . . . . *ib.*
———– O God, thou art my God . . . . *ib.*
———– Lord, how long wilt thou be angry . . . . . *ib.*
———– O God, thou hast cast us out . . . . *ib.*
———– Save me, O God . . . . *ib.*
The whole Service in B flat . . . . **IV.**
Anthem. O give thanks . . . . *ib.*
———– Behold, I bring you glad tidings . . . . *ib.*
———– Be merciful unto me . . . . *ib.*
———– Blessed is the man . . . . *ib.*
———– Thou knowest, O Lord (for the funeral of Queen Mary). *ib.*
The Morning Service in D major . . . . **V.**

RAMSEY (JOHN). The whole Service in F . . . . **IV.**
Some of the Canons at the end of Vol. I. have Ramsey's name
prefixed, but erroneously.

RICHARDSON (VAUGHAN).
Anthem. O Lord God of my salvation . . . . **V.**
The Evening Service in C. (A.D. 1713.) . . . . **VI.**

ROGERS (BENJAMIN).
The Morning and Evening Service in D major . . . . **II.**

No 98

Anthem.   Behold, now praise the Lord   . . . .   Vol. **V.**
————   Lord, thou hast been our refuge   . . . .   *ib.*
————   The Lord is righteous   . . . .   *ib.*
The Morning and Evening Service in E major   . . . .   *ib.*
TYE (CHRISTOPHER).
    The Evening Service in G minor   . . . .   **I.**
    O God, be merciful unto us   . . . .   **IV.**
    O Lord, deliver me from mine enemies   . . . .   *ib.*
WALKLY (ANTHONY). The Morning Service in E flat   . . . . .   **VI.**
WANLESS (THOMAS). Anthem. Awake up my glory   . . . . .   **V.**
WEELKES (THOMAS).
    Anthem. O God, grant the King a long life   . . . .   **III.**
WELDON (JOHN). Anthem. Hear my crying, O God   . . . . .   **V.**
WILDBORE (ROBERT or JOHN). Anthem. Almighty and everlasting
God   . . . .   **IV.**
WILLIAMS (THOMAS). The Evening Service in A minor   . . . .   **V.**
WILKINSON (THOMAS).
    Anthem. O Lord God, my salvation   . . . .   **IV.**
    ————   I am the resurrection   . . . .   *ib.*

WISE (MICHAEL).
    The Morning and Evening Service in D minor   . . . .   **II.**
    Anthem. Awake, put on thy strength   . . . .   *ib.*
    ————   The ways of Zion do mourn   . . . . . .   *ib.*
    ————   How are the mighty fallen   . . . .   **III.**
    ————   I will sing a new song   . . . .   *ib.*
    ————   O praise God in his holiness   . . . .   *ib.*
    ————   Behold how good and joyful .   . . .   *ib.*
    The Evening Service in E flat   . . . .   *ib.*

WHITE (MATTHEW).
    Anthem. O praise God in his holiness   . . . .   **III.**
    ————   The Lord bless us and keep us .   . . .   *ib.*
    The music of this Anthem is the same as one of those in Vol.
II., said to have been adapted to English words by Dr. Aldrich
(*see* " O Lord rebuke me not ") from the works of Palestrina, &c.

WOOLCOT (CHARLES).
    The Morning Service in G major   . . . .   **V.**
    Anthem. O Lord, thou hast cast us out   . . . .   *ib.*

At the end of Vol. I. are the following Canons, the composers of which are not ascertained.

O that men would therefore praise the Lord. (To this Dr. Tudway has
prefixed the name of Thomas Morley, but his authority cannot be de-
pended upon.)
Music divine, the mirror of the arts.
Miserere mei, Domine.

In the *Additional Mss.* No. 11,587 and 11,589, is a Catalogue, in musical notation, of this collection, with remarks
on the several compositions, by Dr. Burney.
6 vols. Quarto. A.D. 1715 to 1720. [*Harl. Mss.* 7337–7342.]

99.

A single voice part of a collection of French, Italian, and
English Songs and Psalms. It formerly belonged to John

Duke of Newcastle, whose engraved book-plate appears inside the cover.

Divin objet, qui ravisses les sens . . . . fol. 5		Avant le moment bien heureux . . . . . . fol. 21		
Se voi, luci amate 6		Si mes soupirs sont indiscrets . 22		
La vita alberga 7		Sure 'twas a dreame 23		
Tell me, you wandering spirits 8		Je ne cognois que trop . . . 24		
Our ears have heard . . . . 8 b.		Non mi date più pene . . . 24 b.		
S'io moro, che dira 9		Amys, si vous me voules croire . 26		
Fanciulla son io 10		Alla cathia pastore 27		
A chi, lasso, credero 11		Je te quitte, Sylure 28		
Amys, qu'on se reveille . . . 12		Si tochi tambura . . . . . 28 b.		
N'entendes vous pas 13				
Blessed are they that perfect are 14		Reversing the volume, are the following:		
Repicavan las campanilias . . 15				
Cloris est belle . . . . . . 15 b.		Ye men on earth. 66th Psalm. f. 7 b.		
Ye children, which doe serve . 16		All people that on earth doe dwell.		
Enfans de Bacchus, mes amys . 17		100th Psalm . . . . . . 8 b.		
Con bell sigilla 18		Sing ye with praise. New tune.		
When shall I see my captive hart 19		96th Psalm . . . . . . 9 b.		
A toy, gros hour soufle . . . 20		Go tell my most malicious fate. (Em. Heath.) . . . . . 10 b.		

Oblong Quarto. xviith cent. [*Harl. Mss.* 7549.]

100.

Fragments of old Songs and Church Music of the time of Henry VIII. and Elizabeth, described by Wanley as " containing a collection of old Songs, etc., used within and about the bishoprick of Durham ";—a single voice part only, and very much mutilated. The names of these composers are given, H. Astone, Mr. Heath, Mr. More, Robert Johnson, and William Mundye. The following are the titles of the pieces.

Lytelle byrdes flatterith most (imperfect) . . . . . fol. 84		In Creat, when Dedylus fyrst began . . . . . fol. 103
My lady is a prety on . . . 85		Rejoyse, O prysoners (no musical notes) . . . . . . 103 b.
Ave, Domyna, Sancta Marya, moost myghtfulle myrrore. (H. Astone.) . . . . . 86 b.		Erravi, sicut oves 104
		Ad Dominum, cum tribularer. (Mr. More.) . . . . . 104 b.
Why dyde the gentels frett and fume. 89		Sagitte potentes 105
Ponder my wordes, O Lorde . 90		If I be wanton, I wotte welle why . . . . 106 b.
Geve to the Lorde, ye potentates . . . . 91 b.		Alone walking and oft musing 106
When truth is tryed . . . 93 b.		Ty the mare, tomboy. (Rob. Johnson.) 111
O come, let us synge unto the Lord 94		Printed by Ritson, ib. p. 130.
I, wofull wretchyd wight . . 95 b.		Aryse, aryse, I say 114
Te Deum. We knowlege thee 98		That of wysse men . . . . 114 b.
Hey downe, downe. (Qd. Mr. Heath.) . . . . . . 100 b.		Houghe the tankerd . . . 115 b.
Printed by Ritson, *Antient Songs*, 1790, p. 134.		What tyme Appelles . . . 116
		I may well banne . . . . ib.
		Take hede bytyme . . . . 116 b.

Folio. xvith cent. [*Harl. Mss.* 7578.]

Bound up in the same volume are some pieces for the
lute, of the xviith cent., amongst which is a Galliard by J.
Coperario, fol. 120 b., and another by Alfonso Ferabosco,
fol. 121.

101.

An Antiphonary, in Latin, splendidly written, having the
initial letters beautifully painted. The volume is supposed,
from the form of the musical notes, to have been written in
Germany. It is imperfect at the end. Vellum. Large
Folio. xvth cent. [*Lansd. Mss.* 460.]

102.

Latin Breviary, with musical notes, according to the use of
Salisbury. Imperfect at the beginning and end. Vellum.
Large Folio. Early part of the xvth cent. [*Lansd. Mss.* 461.]

103.

A Latin Antiphonary according to the use of Salisbury. Imperfect at the commencement. On some spare leaves at the
beginning and the end are Hymns, with " Kyrie eleison,"
etc., in a later hand. Vellum. Large Folio. Early part of
the xvth cent. [*Lansd. Mss.* 462.]

104.

A Latin Service Book according to the use of Salisbury. Imperfect at the beginning and end. Vellum. Large Folio.
Early part of the xvth cent. [*Lansd. Mss.* 463.]

In all probability, this and the three preceding volumes
belonged to the cathedral church of Norwich.

105.

A volume known by the name of The Manuscript of Waltham
Holy Cross Abbey, compiled from the works of various
authors, and transcribed by John Wylde, Precentor of the
said abbey. It is fully described in the general Catalogue
of the Lansdowne Manuscripts, and also analysed and
commented on at great length by Dr. Burney and Sir
John Hawkins in their Histories of Music. The following
is a brief recapitulation of its contents.

" Musica Gwydonis Monachi, Monacordum dicta." A Treatise chiefly
    founded upon the writings of Guido Aretinus, divided into two
    parts, " Musica Manualis " and " Tonale," and probably compiled
    by John Wylde. The prologue begins, " Quia juxta sapientissimum
    Salomonem," and the first chapter, " Hujus artis inventorem " .   fol. 1

At the dissolution of Waltham Abbey this volume appears to have fallen into the bands of Thomas Tallis, Gen-
tleman of the Chapel Royal in the time of K. Henry VIII.
and during the three succeeding reigns. His name (no
doubt an autograph) is upon the last leaf. Vellum. Quarto.
xvth cent. [*Lansd. Mss.* 763]

At the end of the above *Lansdowne Ms.* (of which there is
a modern transcript in *Add. Ms. 4912*) is inserted a letter
from Dr. John Wallis, with remarks on an ancient Greek Ms.
containing a collection of Hymns and Anthems composed for
the use of the Greek church at Constantinople, with an account of the art of singing, musical notes, etc. This is followed by a more detailed description of the Ms., drawn up by

G

Wanley, in whose possession it then was, and by whom it was offered for sale to the Bodleian Library in 1698. See Hawkins's *Hist. of Musick,* vol. i. p. 392. A similar treatise on the Greek musical notes may be found in the *Harl. Ms.* 5544.

106.

Fragments of Songs from a Play called "The Buggbears."

Lend me, you lovers all (apparently a Solo with Chorus) . . . . fol. 75
My sowre is turnd to sweete (a Solo) . . . . *ib.*
Sith all our greafe is turnde to blyss (for three voices; imperfect) . . 75 *b.*

From the rests at the commencement of the Songs it is probable that there was an accompaniment for instruments, or that other voices are wanting to fill up the same. Folio. Latter part of the xvith cent. [*Lansd. Mss.* 807.]

107.

The five books of Boethius "De Musica," beautifully tran-scribed and illuminated, but here divided into three books. Vellum. Large Folio. Early part of the xivth cent. [*Burney Mss.* 275. p. 714.]

Printed with emendations, by Glareanus. fol. Basil. 1570.

108.

A Hymn to Saint James of Persia, in Greek, with the musical notation. Begin. Ἐθαυμαστώθης, Ιακωβε. fol. 6. Vellum. Folio. xiiith cent.

The cxxxiv. Psalm in Greek, with musical notation (imper-fect). fol. 7. Duodecimo. xvith cent. [*Burney Mss.* 276.]

109.

A Hymn, apparently in harmony of two parts. Begin. "Amor Patris et Filii." Vellum. Small Folio. xiiith cent. [*Bur-ney Mss.* 557. p. 30.]

11ᵗʰ Century

110.

Extracts from the "Musica Disciplina" of Aurelianus Reo-mensis. fol. 1.

Printed. by Gerbertus, *Script. Eccles. de Musica,* vol. i. p. 29.

"Musicalis Institucio, a Boetio in Latinum translata de Greco"; in five books. fol. 6 *b.*

Printed amongst the works of Boethius, fol. Basil. 1570.

" Scoliea Enchiriadis de musica," by Ubaldus, or Hucbaldus, Monk of St. Amand, near Valenciennes. fol. 63 *b*.

    Printed by Gerbertus, *Script. Eccles. de Musica*, vol. i. p. 152.

A Treatise on Music, by Berno, Abbot of Reichenau, in the diocese of Constance, (who died A.D. 1048,) intitled " Tonarius." Begin. " Omnis igitur regularis monocordi constitutio." fol. 87 *b*.

    Printed by Gerbertus, *ib.* vol. ii. p. 63, with the addition of a prefatory address, not in the Ms.

    Vellum. Folio. xith cent. [*Arund. Mss.* 77.]

111.

A Latin Breviary according to the use of Salisbury, with musical notes. fol. 1.

" Metrologus liber de plana musica;" very faultily written. *Secreta Bodl 144 fol 78.* fol. 100.

    See another copy in *Lansdowne Ms.* 763. fol. 60. *See Addit. 4912 copied from Lansdowne*

    Vellum. Folio. Written for Henry Percy, Earl of Northumberland, between the years 1446-1461. ' [*Arund. Mss.* 130.]

112.

Hymns, with musical notation, in Latin, French, and English.

O labilis, o flebilis hominis condicio . . . . fol. 153
Magdalene, Laudes plene . . . . 153 *b*.
Cantus de Domina, post cantum Aalis, in Latin and French. Begin.
    " Flos pudicicie . Flur de virginite " . . . . *ib*.
Angelus ad Virginem. (Hymn for the Annunciation) 154
The milde Lomb isprad,o rode. (Hymn on the Crucifixion) . . . . *ib*.
Worldes blis ne last no throwe . . . . *ib*.
Spei vena, melle plena. (Verses on M. Magdalen) . . . . 154 *b*.
Jesu Christes milde moder stud. (A translation of the Hymn " Stabat Mater.") . . . . *ib*.
Salve Virgo Virginum 155
Veine pleine de ducur . . . . *ib*.
Bien deust chanter. (In praise of the Virgin) . . . . *ib*.
Alleluya. Virga ferax . . . . 200 *b*.
Risum facit. (Harmony of 2 parts?) . . . . 201 *b*.

    Vellum. Quarto. xiiith cent. [*Arundel Mss.* 248.]

113.

A Tract on Music. Begin. " Expedit et consonum est racioni." With examples in the eight tones. fol. 32.

A Tract on Music. Begin. " Volentibus ad musice artis noticiam." fol. 80.

    Small Quarto. End of xvth cent. [*Arundel Mss.* 299.]

114.

Various Treatises on Music, chiefly by Guido Aretinus.
"Micrologus Guidonis, de arte musica." fol. 97.
> Printed by Gerbertus, *Script. Eccles. de Musica*, vol. ii.
> p. 2.

"Rithmi ejusdem;" written as prose. fol. 103.
> Printed by Gerbertus, *ib.* vol. ii. p. 25.

Rules of Guido "de ignoto cantu:" Begin. "Temporibus
nostris super omnes." fol. 104.
> Printed by Gerbertus, *ib.* vol. ii. p. 34.

"Epistola Guidonis ad Michahelem monachum." (See
Harl. Ms. 281 and 3199.) fol. 106.
> Printed by Gerbertus, *ib.* vol. ii. p. 43.

"De mensura fistularum." Begin. "Fistularum mensura,
ut a quibusdam." fol. 108 *b.*

"Organistrum." Begin. "Organicam quicunque liram."
fol. 109.
Vellum. Quarto. xiiith cent. [*Arundel Mss.* 339.]

115.

A Book of Latin Hymns for the Festivals throughout the year,
set to music in old notation without lines. Vellum. Small
Quarto. xiiith cent. [*Arundel Mss.* 340.]

116.

A Table of Weights. Begin. "As habet uncias duodecim,"
set to music in old notation. Vellum. Octavo. xith cent.
[*Arundel Mss.* 356. fol. 45.]

117.

Music on a stave of six lines, with the three clefs F, C, and G
marked at their relative distances, to the words "Pulchra es,
amica mia." Vellum. Small Quarto. xiiith cent. [*Arundel.
Mss.* 505. fol. 50.]

118.

A collection of Hymns sung in the principal festivals of the
Greek Church, from September to April, adapted to musical
notes by Johannes Cucuzelus. Among these Hymns are
some attributed to other authors, as Johannes Lampadarius,
Georgius Sguropulus, and Manuel Chrysaphes. Small
Quarto. xvth cent. [*Arund. Mss.* 527.]

119.

A volume containing the second, third, and fourth Concertos of George Frederic Handel, in score, in the handwriting of the composer, signed at the end " G. F. H., March 25, 1735." The third Concerto differs in some parts from the copies afterwards printed, and may therefore be the first sketch. The fourth concludes with a vocal chorus to the word Hallelujah, upon a subject resembling the last movement of the said Concerto, and which the composer afterwards introduced in his Oratorio of " Time and Truth." Quarto. [*George III. Mss.* 317.]

120.

" Concert of antient vocal and instrumental music, established A.D. 1776, with a catalogue of the several pieces performed since its institution " [to the year 1792]. Quarto. [*George III. Mss.* 318.

121.

" Recueil de Chansons choisies en Vaudevilles, pour servir a l'histoire anecdote, depuis 1600 jusqu'à 1749." To each volume is annexed an alphabetical table of names in connexion with the poetry. The music consists of French airs, mostly of an early date. 8 Vols. Quarto. [*George III. Mss.* 330-337.]

There is a more complete copy of this very curious collection in the *Egerton Mss.* 814-817.

122.

" Dicta Philippi [de Greve], quondam Cancellarii Parisiensis ; " consisting of Latin Hymns, moral and satirical verses, etc. adapted to music ; also French Songs, the poetry by Colard le Boutillier, Messire Raouls, Jehan de Nuefville, Messire Gasses Brulez, and Messire Regnaut, Castellain de Couchy.

Ave gloriosa virginum	fol. 3
O Maria, virginei flos. (*De Beata Maria*)	7 b.
Inter membra singula. (*Disputatio membrorum*)	12
This is the fable of the members rebelling against the belly.	
Homo, vide que. (*Angaria Christi in cruce*)	20
O mens, cogita. (*De miseria hominis*)	20 b.
Homo, considera. (*De miseria hominis*)	22 b.
Quisquis cordis. (*Disputatio cordis et oculi*)	24 b.
Nitimur in vetitum. (*De reprehensione hominis*)	25 b.
Pater sancte, dictus. (*De Innocentie pontifice*)	26 b.
Cum sit omnis caro fenum	27 b.
Veritas, equitas. (*De prelatis*)	28 b.

After these follow Latin Hymns for the festivals of Palm Sunday, the Purification of the Virgin, St. Mark, etc., with musical notes, and directions where they should be sung; all written by a later hand . 132 b.

Note.—The pieces marked thus (*) are by a later hand of the xvth cent., which has barbarously written over and partly erased the original French songs.

Vellum. Duodecimo. End of the xiiith cent. [*Egerton Mss. 274.*]

123.

A Treatise on Music, by Isidore, Bishop of Seville, who wrote in the seventh century. Begin. " Musica est peritia modulationis." Originally in nine chapters, but the present copy completed only as far as the middle of the eighth. Vellum. Folio. End of the xiiith cent. [*Egerton Mss.* 630. fol. 224 *b.*]
Printed by Gerbertus, *Script. Eccles. de Musica*, vol. i. p. 19.

124.

" Chansonnier, ou Recueil de Chansons annecdotées, depuis l'annéc 1600 jusqu'à present, 1744." 4 Vols. Quarto. [*Egerton Mss.* 814–817.]
See a more complete copy in *George III. Mss.* 330–337.

125.

An Icelandic Service Book, with musical notes. A later hand has added Psalms and Hymns for different occasions. Folio. xvith cent. [*Sloane Mss.* 503.]

126.

A miscellaneous musical collection, containing the tablature with exercises for the lute, instructions on music in general, etc., with a variety of curious pen and ink drawings; also songs, quotations, and annotations in Latin and German, neatly transcribed by Johannes Stobæus, Chapel Master to the Elector of Brandenburg. Quarto. Dated Regiomonti, A.D. 1640. [*Sloane Mss.* 1021.]

127.

A volume of Muscovite Hymns, with musical notes; stated in the Ms. Sloane Catalogue to have been bought in Moscow, A.D. 1662. Duodecimo. xviith cent. [*Sloane Mss.* 1335.]

128.

Original Letters from John Baynard, John Carr, and John Heptinstall, to Dr. William Holder, relative to the publication of his Treatise on Harmony, in 1692–1694. Quarto. [*Sloane Mss.* 1388. fol. 55.]

129.

An original warrant of Queen Elizabeth to " Thomas Gyles, maister of the children of the cathedrall churche of St. Paule, within our cittie of London, to take upp suche apte and

meete children as are most fitt to be instructed and framed in
the arte and science of musicke and singinge, as may be had
and founde out within anie place of this our realme of England or Wales." Dated "Grenewich, 26 day of Aprill, iu
the xxviith yeare of our reign." A.D. 1585. [*Sloane Mss.*
2035. fol. 116.]

130.

"Prælectiones Musicæ in Ædibus Gresham," by John Taverner, in the year 1610. These lectures, nine in number, are
partly in Latin and partly in English, and are in the author's
handwriting. Quarto. [*Sloane Mss.* 2329.]

131.

A small Latin Service Book, with musical notes. Duodecimo.
xvith cent. [*Sloane Mss.* 2637.]

132.

Allemands, Gigues, Corantes, Sarabands, etc., in tablature
similar to that for the lute; in the handwriting of J. A.
Kæmpfer. Oblong Quarto. xviith cent. [*Sloane Mss.* 2923.
ff. 3–36.]

133.

"An essay tending to the making out a probability of guesse
and conjecture att the temperature and disposition, by the
severall musicall modulations of the voyce in ordinary speech
and discourse." Quarto. xviith cent. [*Sloane Mss.* 3087.
fol. 32.]

134.

A volume, very neatly transcribed, containing Turkish, Persian,
and Arabic Songs. Annexed to the book is a complete index
in Latin, according to which the original cover bore the following inscription, "Dominus ac Poss^or. Ali Beg Essan-
turi sive Cymbalista a musicis Imperatoris Mahummedi," anno
1060[?]. Oblong Quarto. xviith cent. [*Sloane Mss.* 3114.]

135.

A book bearing the name of Charles Cavendysshe, containing
some pieces of music in two parts, without words. Oblong
Quarto. xviith cent. [*Sloane Mss.* 3992.]

136.

Two letters addressed to Sir Hans Sloane, in 1705–6, by Thomas Salmon, respecting music. It is presumed this is the same Thomas Salmon who, in 1672, published an essay for simplifying music by reducing all the cleffs to one universal character. Folio. [*Sloane Mss.* 4058. fol. 109.]

137.

Fragment of a collection of Hymns for the service of the Greek Church, with musical notes; some of which were composed by Manuel Chrysaphes and Johannes Lampadarius. Duodecimo. xvth cent. [*Sloane Mss.* 4087.]

138.

Miscellaneous notes and calculations, chiefly relating to the scale of music proposed by John Birchensha. fol. 1.

" Compendium musicæ. Bredæ Brabantinorum, pridie Calendas Januarias, anno 1618 completo." At the end is the following note : " Hic libellus fuit paulo post hanc excriptionem typis impressus, preposito hoc titulo, Renati Des Cartes Musicæ compendium, Trajecti ad Rhenum, anno 1650, in quarto." fol. 33.

A printed sheet, being an " Animadversion," by John Birchensha, of a book about to be published by him, intitled "Syntagma musicæ." fol. 47.

" Psalme 100 [harmonized] by John Dowland, Doctor of Musicke." fol. 52.

" Grieve not, deare love," an air by Henry Lawes. fol. 54.

" Amor vittorioso," and " La sirena." Two balletti without words. fol. 54.

Rough notes, etc., concerning the theory of music. fol. 61. Folio. xviith cent. [*Add. Mss.* 4388.]

139.

Directions " to make chimes." Folio. Dated 18 Feb. 163$\frac{1}{4}$. [*Add. Mss.* 4459. fol. 18 *b*.]

140.

Songs, some with words, others with the lute part only. The names of the following composers are given : John Heywoode, John Taverner, John Shepherde, Robert Johnson, and Thomas Tallis.

Folio. xviith cent. [*Add. Mss.* 4900.]

141.

A volume containing Treatises on Music, being a copy made for Dr. Pepusch of part of Tiberius, B. ix. in the Cottonian Library, which part was subsequently destroyed by fire.

" Regulæ cum maximis Magistri Franconis, cum additionibus aliorum musicorum, compilata a Roberto de Handlo " . . . . p. 1

> Thomas Morley, in the Annotations on his Introduction to Music, 1597, says " Franco is the most ancient of all those whose works of practical music have come to my hands; one Roberto de Haulo [Handlo] hath made as it were commentaries upon his rules, and termed them additions." Handlo's Commentaries bear date 1326, and Franco, who was scholastic of Liege, wrote in the latter half of the twelfth century. It contains a very full account of the ancient notes, ligatures, etc. Begin. " *Franco.* Gaudent brevitate moderni, etc. *Handlo.* Erectæ longæ sive perfectæ sint."
> See Gerbertus, *Script. Eccles. de Musica,* vol. iii. p. 1.

" Incipit tractatus diversarum Figurarum, per quas dulces modi discantantur, et ideo sequendo ordinem tenoris, scilicet alterius temporis, secundum Egidium [Johannem] de Muris vel de Morino," etc. A treatise founded on the works of John De Muris 23

> See Gerbertus, *ib.* vol. iii. p. 190.

An anonymous Treatise on the science of Music in general, founded on the writings of Boetius, Guido, and Franco. Begin. " Pro aliqua notitia de musica habenda." 34

Another anonymous Treatise, begin. " Cognita modulatione melorum." 112

Another anonymous Treatise, begin. " Est autem unisonus." 133

Another anonymous Treatise, begin. " Cum in isto tractatu." 195

> See other copies of these three treatises in *Ms. Reg.* 12 c. vi.

Folio. Early part of the xviiith cent. [*Add. Mss.* 4909.]

A full account of this volume is given in Sir J. Hawkins's *History of Music,* vol. ii. pp. 175-201.

142.

A volume containing:

Extracts from Dethlevus Cluverus, " Disquisitiones Philosophicæ, oder, Historische Anmerckungen," etc. 2d pt. 4to. Hamb. 1711; in *German*. fol. 1.

An anonymous Latin treatise, begin. " Sonus consideratus in genere." fol. 12. End of xviith cent.

" A collection of rules in musicke from the most knowing masters in that science, with Mr. Birchensha's six rules of composition, and his enlargement thereon, to the Right Honble. William Lord Viscount Brouncker, etc., collected by mee, Silas Domvill als. Taylor; " written about 1669. fol. 41.

The other masters named are Christopher Simpson and Matthew Locke, by the latter of whom, at fol. 45, are rules for playing from a basso continuo, and at fol. 68, two Canons in three parts. Silas Taylor was an intimate friend of M. Locke, and is better known as the author of a " History of Gavelkind."

" Tractat von der Musicalischen Composition," by N. N. Böhmer, organist of St. Michael's Church in Luneburg. fol. 70. xviiith cent.

Folio. [*Add. Mss.* 1910.]

143.

A volume in Scottish orthography, intitled " The Art of Music collecit out of all ancient Doctouris of Music." Begin. " Qubat is mensural music?" On the first page is written, in a more recent hand, " Liber Collegii Musæi Minervæ, ex dono Fra. Kinaston, Reg^tis. 1635." Folio. xvith cent. [*Add. Mss.* 1911.]

144.

A transcript made for Dr. Pepusch of the Manuscript No. 763 in the Lansdowne collection, commonly called the Manuscript of Waltham Holy Cross Abbey. Folio. Early part of the xviiith cent. [*Add. Mss.* 1912.]

See N.º 105

145.

" Theorica Musice Franchini Gafuri, Laudensis "; in five books, dedicated to Lodovico Maria Sforza, Duke of Bari. Folio. End of the xvth cent. [*Add. Mss.* 1913.]

This work was printed at Naples, in 1480.

146.

" Brevis Musicæ Isagoge, Joanne Frisio,· Tigurino, Authore;
accesserunt priori editioni omnia Horatii carminum genera;
item Heroica, Elegiaca, etc., quatuor vocibus ad æquales, in
studiosorum adolescentum gratiam composita. Tiguri, apud
Frosch[ium], 1555." Quarto. xviiith cent. [*Add. Mss.*
4914.]

The original printed copy of this work contains only one
out of the four equal voice parts. This Manuscript having
them in partition is therefore more complete. It appears by
the preface to the printed book, that the tenor part was the
only one composed by Frisins, the other three being added
by his friend Henricus Textor, and probably published separately at a later period.

147.

A volume containing Treatises on Music, by Guido Aretinus
and others; copied from a manuscript in Baliol College,
Oxon.

" Micrologus, id est brevis sermo in musica, editus a domino Guidone, piissimo
monacho, et peritissimo musico." p. 1.
It agrees with the copy printed in Gerbertus, *Script. Eccles. de Musica*,
vol. ii. pp. 2-24.
The " Regulæ Rhythmicæ " of Guido (written here as prose); with the five
prefatory verses. p. 33.
Printed *ib.* vol. ii. pp. 25-33.
The Rules " de ignoto cantu," by the same. p. 42.
Printed *ib.* vol. ii. pp. 34-37.
" Epistola Guidonis ad amicum suum." p. 47.
Printed *ib.* vol. ii. pp. 43-50.
Dialogue on Music, attributed to Oddo, Abbot of Cluny. Begin. " Quid est
musica? Veraciter canendi scientia." (See *Harl. Ms.* 281.) p. 62.
Printed *ib.* vol. i. pp. 252-264.
The Prologue to the " Tonarius " of Berno, Abbot of Reichenau, addressed
" Domino Deoque dilecto Piligrino." p. 85.
Printed *ib.* vol. ii. pp. 62-79.

Quarto. xviiith cent. [*Add. Mss.* 4915.]

148.

A tract containing extracts from Isaac Casaubon's Latin version
of Athenæus, edit. Lugd. 1657; chiefly on ancient musical
instruments. Quarto. xviiith cent. [*Add. Mss.* 4916.]

149.

" Observations concerning Musick, made anno Domini 1705
or 1706, by the Rev. Mr. Bedford, Chaplain to the Haber-
dashers' Hospital, at Hoxton, near London." Small Quarto.
[*Add. Mss.* 4917.]

150.

" Traité de la Musique moderne, avec quelques remarques sur la musique ancienne, par A. D. V., 1702." According to the preface, this treatise should consist of three parts, but the first part only is in Manuscript. Small Quarto. [*Add. Mss.* 4918.]

151.

" The practicall theory of Musick, to perform musick in perfeet proportions, and to set out the proportions upon the viol, so that they may fall right upon the frets, 1702." Small Quarto. [*Add. Mss.* 4919.]

152.

" Utile et breve regule di canto, composite per Maestro Zoanne di Spadari, da Bologna." Begin. " Nel canto figurato overo mensurato." Small Quarto. Written in the year 1510. [*Add. Mss.* 4920.]

153.

" An abstract of the accounts the Royal Society has given of the Authors who have wrote upon Music, that have appeared since the first institution by King Charles, to the present time, in their works intitled ' The Philosophical Transactions;' by James Grassineau, 1743." Small Quarto. [*Add. Mss.* 4921.]

154.

" Regole per il contrappunto." At the end is a piece of music in four parts, by Giovanni Bernardino Nanino, which renders it probable that this Manuscript is copied from a work published towards the end of the sixteenth century, intitled " Trattato di contrappunto, con la Regola per far contrappunto." Small Quarto. xviith cent. [*Add. Mss.* 4922.]

155.

" Tractatus de Musica." Begin. " Musicam non incongrue definieris." Duodecimo. xviith cent. [*Add. Mss.* 4923.]

The following twenty-eight volumes, numbered 5036 to 5062, were almost entirely transcribed from the Libraries at Oxford, about the middle of the eighteenth century, by

Henry Needler, of the Excise Office, whose widow presented them to James Mathias, by whom they were bequeathed to the Trustees of the British Museum, in 1782.

156.

Motetts, Masses, and Madrigals, in score, for five and six voices, composed by Giov. Pier Luigi da Palestrina (here called J. P. A. Prænestini), T. L. de Victoria, Orlando di Lasso, Alfonso Ferabosco, senior, Edvardus Lupus, and Andreas Pevernage.

Quarto. Middle of the xviiith cent. [*Add. Mss.* 5036.]

157.

A volume containing the following music, by Giov. Pier Luigi da Palestrina:

1st pagination. Motetts for five voices, in score, for several Sundays and festivals.

2nd pagination. Motetts for several festivals, and parts of Masses, for two, three, four, and five voices.

Quarto. Middle of the xviiith cent. [*Add. Mss.* 5037.]

158.

Motetts for various festivals, etc., and a mass, in score, for four voices, by Giov. Pier Luigi da Palestrina.

Quarto. Middle of the xviiith cent. [*Add. Mss.* 5038.]

159.

" Delli Madrigali spirituali a cinque voci, di Gio. Pietro Luigi
Prenestino [Palestrina], Maestro di Capella di St. Pietro di
Roma, 1594." The dedication to the Grand Duchess of
Tuscany of the original printed parts from which this score
is made, bears date " Di Roma, il primo giorno del anno
1594." The work must therefore have been the composer's
last, as he died in February of the same year.

Quarto.   Middle of the xviiith cent.   [*Add. Mss.* 5039.]

160.

" Messe a quatro voci del Palestrina, cioè, *Di Papa Marcello*,
ridotta à 4 da Gio. Francesco Anerio; *Iste Confessor*, et
Sine nomine; e la quarta *Della Battaglia* è del istesso Gio.
Franc. Anerio; con il basso continuo per l'organo, di novo
diligimente corretta da Francesco Gannini.   In Roma,
1689."

The above named Mass " *Di Papa Marcello* " (originally
in six parts), is the one which so delighted the Pope (A.D.
1555), who had previously determined to suppress ecclesiastical music, that in consequence thereof it was restored to
favour.

Quarto.   Middle of the xviiith cent.   [*Add. Mss.* 5040.]

161.

" Messe dell' Abbate Dominico dal Pane, Soprano della Capella Pontificia, a quatro, cinque, sei, et otto voci, estratte
da esquisiti Motetti del Palestrina.   Opera quinta, in Roma,
1687."

The following are the titles of the Motetts by Palestrina,
which are herein adapted to the words of the Mass.

Doctor bonus. Four voices . p. 1	O beatum virum. Five voices. p. 88
Domine, quando veneris. Four	Jubilate Deo. Five voices . . 132
voices 27	Canite tuba in Sion. Six voices 170
Stella quam viderant magi. Five	Fratres ego enim accepi. Eight
voices 51	voices 218

Quarto. Middle of the xviiith cent. [*Add. Mss.* 5041.]

162.

A volume containing copies, in score, of the following printed works of Orlando di Lasso :

1. " Novæ aliquot et ante hac non ita usitatæ ad duas voces Cantiones suavissimæ, authore Orlando di Lasso, Illustrissimi Bavariæ Ducis Alberti Musici Chori Magistro. Londini, excudebat Thomas Este, 1598."

2. " Moduli nondum prius editi Monachii Boioariæ, ternis vocibus, ab Orlando Lasso compositi. Lutetiæ Parisiorum, 1576."

3. " Sacræ Lectiones novem ex Propheta Job, quatuor vocum, Autore Orlando Lasso. Noribergæ, 1575."

Quarto. Middle of the xviiith cent. [*Add. Mss.* 5042.]

163.

A copy, in score, of the following printed work :

" Joannis Mouton, Sameracensis, musici præstantissimi, selecti aliquot Moduli, et in 4, 5, 6, et 8 vocum harmoniam distincti. Liber Primus. Parisiis, 1555."

Quarto. Middle of the xviiith cent. [*Add. Mss.* 5043.]

164.

A volume containing the following Motetts and a Mass, in full score, for five voices, with instrumental accompaniments, by Giov. Battista Pergolesi.

Laudate Pueri . . . . . . p. 1	Stabat Mater . . . . . p. 143
Confitebor tibi, Domine . . . 69	Salve Regina 194
Domine, ad adjuvandum . . . 120	Messa 211

The " Salve Regina " was Pergolesi's last work, A.D. 1737. Quarto. Middle of the xviiith cent. [*Add. Mss.* 5044.]

165.

" Joannis Petri Loysii Prænestini, in Basilica Sti. Petri de Urbe Capellæ Magistri, Missarum Liber Primus. Romæ, 1572."

This is a copy, in score, of one of Palestrina's most celebrated works. It was first published in very large folio,

having all the voice parts printed in such a manner as to
admit of being sung at one view from the same book, in-
stead of being in separate volumes, as was usually the case
at that period; and on the title was a curious wood engrav-
ing representing the composer on his knees, in the act of
exhibiting a copy of his book to the reigning Pope, Julius III.
The following are the titles of the Masses:

Ecce sacerdos magnus. Four voices . . . . p. 1		Gabriel Archangelus. Four voices . . . . p. 100	
O Regem cœli. Four voices . . 32		Ad cœnam Agni. Five voices . 120	
Viveste magna. Four voices . 91			

Quarto. Middle of the XVIIIth cent. [Add. Mss. 5045.]

166.

A copy, in score, of the following printed work:
"Edvardi Lupi, Lusitani, civis Olisiponensis, in metropo-
litana ejusdem urbis ecclesia Beneficiarii, et Musices Præfecti,
Liber Missarum, 4, 5, 6, et 8 vocibus. Antverpiæ, 1621."
Quarto. Middle of the XVIIIth cent. [Add. Mss. 5046.]

167.

A copy, in score, of the following printed work:
"Liber Missarum, 4, 5, et 6 vocibus, authore Thoma
Ludovico à Victoria. Romæ, 1583." With a dedication to
Philip II. of Spain. Quarto. Middle of the XVIIIth cent.
[Add. Mss. 5047.]

168.

"Gloria in excelsis," in full score, for four voices, with instrumental accompaniments, by Sign'. [Domenico Francesco?]
Negri. Quarto. Middle of the XVIIIth cent. [Add. Mss.
5048.]

169.

A volume containing,
1. A "Stabat Mater," in full score, for four voices, with
instrumental accompaniments, composed in the early part of
the eighteenth century, by the Baron Emanuel D'Astorga.
Some part of it is printed in Latrobe's selection of sacred
music.
2. A "Stabat Mater," in full score, for six voices, with accompaniments for two violins, three tenors, and violoncello,
composed by Agostino Steffani, about the end of the 17th
century.
Quarto. Middle of the XVIIIth cent. [Add. Mss. 5049.]

170.

A copy, in score, of the following printed work :

" Il primo libro de Madrigali a cinque voci, de Don Aurelio della Faya, Maestro di Capella della citta di Lanciano. In Venetia, 1564."

Quarto. Middle of the xviiith cent. [*Add. Mss.* 5050.]

171.

A copy, in score, of the following printed work :

" Liber primus Sacrarum Cantionum quinque vocum, vulgo Moteta vocant, ex optimis hujus ætatis musicis selectarum. Antverpiæ, 1546."

Salve, quæ roseo. (Tilem. Susato.) . . . . p. 1	Da mihi, Domine . . . . p. 79
Hunc tibi ille Pater. (*id.*) . . 11	Super flumina. (Benedictus.) . 86
Tulerunt Dominum. (Cadeac.) 19	Adhereat lingua mea. (*id.*) . 99
Et dum ergo fleret. (*id.*) . . 26	O stupor et gaudium 112
In illo tempore. (Tilem. Susato.) 33	Te igitur obsecramus 121
Nondum enim. (*id.*) 41	Non conturbetur 128
Amen dico vobis. (Jo. Castileti.) 48	Ite in orbem 135
	Verbum iniquum 142
Qui manducat. (*id.*) 54	Duo rogavite 149
Ite in orbem. (P. de Manchicourt.) 59	Adjuva nos, Deus. (Thos. Crequillon.) 156
Signa eos. (*id.*) 65	Domine, ne memineris . . . 163
Emitte, Domine 73	Adjuva nos, Deus 171

Quarto. Middle of the xviiith cent. [*Add. Mss.* 5051.]

172.

" Britannia and Augusta, an Ode [for one and two soprano voices, with instrumental accompaniments] after the Italian manner, in honour of the late Duke of Devonshire; written by Mr. John Hughes, set to musick by Mr. John Christian Pepusch." This must have been composed before 1713, as Pepusch in that year took his degree of *Doctor.* Oblong Quarto. Middle of the xviiith cent. [*Add. Mss.* 5052.]

173.

Anthems, with instrumental accompaniments, by Hester Needler, widow of Henry Needler, by whom the collection of Additional Manuscripts, Nos. 5036 to 5062, was almost entirely transcribed. Oblong Quarto. Dated A.D. 1751. [*Add. Mss.* 5053.]

174.

A collection of Motetts, Madrigals, and other pieces, in score, for two, three, four, five, six, seven, and nine voices, by various composers, chiefly of the sixteenth century, viz., William Croft, Agostino Steffani, Thos. Weelkes, W. Damon, Palestrina, Luca Marenzio, Josquin des Pres, Clemens non Papa, Constanza Porta, Ludovico a Victoria, Bonus, Orlando di Lasso, William Byrd, Thos. Tallis, Claude Le Jeune, Robert Fayrfax, Giov. Gero, Gio. Matteo, Gerard Turnhout, Silvestro Durante, William Mundy, Francesco Foggia, Hercole Bernabei, Thos. Morley, Henry Purcell, Johannes Mouton, Dr. Pepusch, and Paolo Petti.

Quarto. Middle of the xviiith cent. [*Add. Mss.* 5054.]

175.

A volume of Duetts, with a bass accompaniment, composed by Agostino Steffani, in the latter part of the seventeenth century.

The last twelve are in the handwriting of John Immyns, who founded the Madrigal Society, 1741.

Quarto. Middle of the XVIIIth cent. [*Add. Mss.* 5055.]

176.

A volume of Duetts, composed in the latter part of the seventeenth century, by the following Italian masters, viz., Agostino Steffani, Pietro Torri, Alessandro Stradella, Francesco Antonio Pistocchi, Feroci, Bernardo Pasquini, and Antonio Lotti.

Troppo cruda. (A. Steffani.)	. . p. 7	Another copy in *Add. Ms.* 5332	
Occhi, perche piangete. (*id.*)	. . . 13	. . . . .	5055 and 5330
Rio destin. (*id.*)	 20	. . . .	*ib.*
Quando un Eroe. (*id.*)	 22	. . . .	5332
O care catene. (*id.*)	 31	. . . .	*ib.*
Quando ti stringo. (*id.*)	 34	. . . .	5330
Combaton. (*id.*)	 38		
Dolce labro. (*id.*)	 40	. . . .	5330
In amarti o bella. (*id.*)	 45	. . . .	*ib.*
Vò dicendo. (*id.*)	 48	. . . .	5331
Voi vene pentirete. (*id.*)	. . . 57	. . . .	*ib.*
Libertà. (*id.*)	 66	. . . .	*ib.*
Turbini tempestosi. (*id.*)	. . . 69	. . . .	*ib.*
Porto ne lumi un mare. (*id.*)	. . . 77	. . . .	5332
Che non sà che cosa. (*id.*)	. . . 82	. . . .	*ib.*
No non voglio. (*id.*)	 85	. . . .	*ib.*
Tien mi il cor. (*id.*)	 90	. . . .	*ib.*
O mia vita. (*id.*)	 93	. . . .	*ib.*
Già tu parti. (*id.*)	 95		
No mai nol diro. (*id.*)	 97	. . . .	5330
Son erede di tormenti. (*id.*)	. . 99	. . . .	*ib.*
Non voglio no. (*id.*)	 105	. . . .	5329
Piagge fiorite. (P. Torri.)	. . . 110	. . . .	5335
Per te, mio bene. (*id.*)	 120	. . . .	*ib.*
Dal arco d'un bel ciglio. (*id.*)	. . 126	. . . .	*ib.*
Odi, O Lilla. (*id.*)	 130	. . . .	*ib.*
Da me lungi. (*id.*)	 140	. . . .	*ib.*
Valli secrete. (*id.*)	 152	. . . .	*ib.*
Vivo in pene. (*id.*)	 156	. . . .	*ib.*
Troppo grave. (A. Stradella.)	. . . 159		
M'incateno Cupido. (F. A. Pistocchi.)	164		
Che sara di te. (Feroci.)	 167		
D'improviso riede il riso. (*id.*)	. . 170		
E destino. (B. Pasquini.)	 173		
Io mi parto. (A. Steffani.)	. . . 177	. . . .	5331
Dolce e per voi. (*id.*)	 185	. . . .	*ib.*
Dolce labro. (*id.*)	 191	. . . .	5330
Conduceti mi verso il porto. (*id.*)	. . 195		
Sol negl'occhi. (*id.*)	 199	. . . .	5330
Ho che lungi. (A. Lotti.)	 207		

Quarto. Middle of the xviiith cent. [*Add. Mss.* 5056.]

177.

A volume of Songs and Duetts, by different composers, about
the middle of the eighteenth century. With accompaniments.

Da te lungi, O volto amato	p. 1
Cara addio. (Gennaro Manna, in Roma, 1748.)	9
Bastan l'affanni miei. (Giov. Cocchi.)	19
Che non mi disse un di. (Giov. Batt. Pergolesi.)	29
Quando saprai chi sono. (Andrea Bernasconi.)	36

Quarto. Middle of the xviiith cent. [*Add. Mss.* 5057.]

178.

A volume of Motetts, in score, for five voices; chiefly, if not entirely, composed by William Byrd, [1589.]

Gaudeamus omnes . . . . p. 1	Apparebit in finem . . . . p. 88
Id. 5	Vigilate, nescitis 94
Precamur, sancte Domine . . 9	In resurrectione tua 103
Tristitia et anxietas . . . 14	Respice, Domine 107
Sed, tu Domine 23	Lætentur cœli 110
De lamentatione Hieremiæ . . 29	Fac cum servo tuo 114
Defecit in dolore 34	Domine, secundum multitudinem 122
Sed tu, Domine 40	Tribulationes civitatum . . . 128
Sordes ejus in pedibus 45	Timor et hebitudo 132
Laudate Dominum 50	Nos enim pro peccatis 138
O vos omnes 59	Quis me statim 143
Domine, tu jurasti 65	Plorans plorabit 148
Audivi vocem de cœlo . . . 73	Dic Regi 151
Defixæ sunt in terram . . . 79	Mirabile misterium 155

Quarto. Middle of the xviiith cent. [*Add. Mss.* 5058.]

179.

A volume of Motetts, in score, for five and six voices, by different English composers of the sixteenth century.

Domine, prestolamur. (W.	Salvator mundi. (Thos. Tal-
Bird.) . . . . . . p. 1	lis.) . . . . p. 13
Attollite portas. (*id.*) . . . 49	Domine, quis habitabit. (*id.*) . 121
Ave, Dei Patris. (Rob. Johnson.) 17	Incipit Lamentatio. (*id.*) . . 137
Aspice, Domine. (Peter Phillips.) 59	De lamentatione Hieremiæ. (*id.*) 149
Miserere mei, Deus. (Christ. Tye.) 71	Absterge Domine. (*id.*) . . 169
O splendor gloriæ. (John Taver-	Sabbatum transisset. (*id.*) . . 179
ner.) 91	

Quarto. Middle of the xviiith cent. [*Add. Mss.* 5059.]

180.

Scales and examples in Harmony, by John Christopher Pepusch. Quarto. Middle of the xviiith cent. [*Add. Mss.* 5060.]

181.

" ' The ways of Zion do mourn ;' an Anthem performed in King Henry the Seventh's Chappel at Westminster, at the funeral of Queen Caroline, on the 17th day of December, 1737. Compos'd by George Frederick Handel." Full score. Oblong Quarto. Middle of the xviiith cent. [*Add. Mss.* 5061.]

182.

"Messiah, an Oratorio, composed by George Frederick Handel." Full score. Oblong Quarto. Middle of the xviiith cent. [*Add. Mss.* 5062.]

183.

"Saul," an Oratorio, in full score, by George Frederick Handel. Folio. Middle of the xviiith cent. [*Add. Mss.* 5319.]

This and the eighteen following volumes, Nos. 5319 to 5337, were presented to the British Museum by Sir John Hawkins, in 1789.

184.

"Israel in Egypt," an Oratorio, in full score, by George Frederick Handel. Large Quarto. Middle of the xviiith cent. [*Add. Mss.* 5320.]

185.

"Acis and Galatea," a Serenata, in full score, by George Frederick Handel. At the end is an Italian Song, " De l'aquila," with an accompaniment for the arch-lute. Oblong Quarto. Middle of the xviiith cent. [*Add. Mss.* 5321.]

186.

Twelve Duetts, by George Frederick Handel. These are printed, and known by the designation of " Chamber Duetts." Oblong Quarto. Middle of the xviiith cent. [*Add. Mss.* 5322.]

187.

"Te Deum and Jubilate" in D major, in full score, by George Frederick Handel. Quarto. Middle of the xviiith cent. [*Add. Mss.* 5323.]

188.

"Phœbe," a Pastoral Drama, in full score, set to music by Dr. Maurice Greene, in the early part of the eighteenth century; the words by Dr. John Hoadly. Oblong Quarto. Middle of the xviiith cent. [*Add. Mss.* 5324.]

189.

"Florimel, or Love's Revenge," a Pastoral Drama, set to music by Dr. Maurice Greene, in the early part of the eighteenth century; the words by Dr. John Hoadly. Oblong Quarto. Middle of the xviiith cent. [*Add. Mss.* 5325.]

190.

" The Song of Deborah and Barak," set to music, in full score, by Dr. Maurice Greene, in the early part of the eighteenth century. Oblong Quarto. Middle of the xviiith cent. [*Add. Mss.* 5326.]

191.

A volume containing the following Anthems, by Dr. Maurice Greene:

The Lord is my strength	. . . p. 1	O give thanks	. . . . .	p. 147
God is our hope	 13	Lord, let me know my end	. .	166
I will give thanks	 36	My soul truly waiteth	. . .	174
I will alway give thanks	. . . 52	Acquaint thyself with God	. .	186
Hear my prayer, O God	. . . 64	O Lord, our Governor	. . .	195
O Lord, give ear	 73	I will magnify thee, O God	. .	210
O God, thou art my God	. . . 84	Lord, how are they increased	.	221
I will seek unto God	 98	O how amiable are thy dwellings		230
Have mercy on me	 100	At the end is a chant by		
Let God arise	 126	Dr. Greene, in B flat.		

Oblong Quarto. Middle of the xviiith cent. [*Add. Mss.* 5327.]

192.

" Hercules," a Serenata, in score, having this inscription at the end : " Finis, John (originally written *Doctor*) Stanley." Quarto. Latter part of the xviiith cent. [*Add. Mss.* 5328.]

193.

Duetts, chiefly for treble and bass, composed by Agostino Steffani, about the end of the seventeenth century.

Sia maledetto amor	. . . . p. 1	Another copy in *Add. Ms.* 5055
Gelosia, che vuoi da me	 17	. . . . ib.
Tengo per infallibile	 31	. . . . ib.
Aure, voi che volate	 46	. . . . ib.
Non voglio	 58	 5056
Siete il più bizarro	 66	
Dir che giovi	 70	 5055
In amor chi vuol godere	 76	
Non te lo dissi	 82	
Luci belle non tanta fretta	. . . 86	
La fortuna su la ruota	 90	
Labri belli	 96	
E spento l'ardore	 102	
Nel tempo ch'amai	 105	 5055
Fulminate, saettate	 107	
Più non amo	 114	
Quel bel foco	 116	

K

Oblong Quarto. Early part of the xviiith cent. [*Add. Mss.* 5329.]

194.

Duetts, for treble and contralto, composed by Agostino Steffani, towards the end of the seventeenth century. Prefixed is a printed " Memoir of the life of Sig. Agostino Steffani, sometime master of the electoral chapel at Hanover, and afterwards Bishop of Spiga," in which is a short detail of Buononcini's plagiarism in regard to Lotti's Madrigal, "In una siepe ombrosa."

Oblong Quarto. Early part of the xviiith cent. [*Add. Mss.* 5330.]

195.

Duetts, for treble and tenor, composed by Agostino Steffani, towards the end of the seventeenth century.

Vò dicendo al mio pensiero	p. 1	Another copy in *Add. Ms.* 5056
E perche non m'uccidete	15	5055
E cosi mi compatite	27	*ib.*
Questo fior	39	*ib.*
Vorrei dire	50	*ib.*
Gelosia, che vuoi da me	62	*ib.*
Ah che l'ò sempre detto	74	*ib.*
Non vene state	89	*ib.*
Quando mai verrà	107	*ib.*
Dolce è per voi soffrire	118	5056
Forma un mare	127	
Se potessi almeno	141	
Il mio seno	154	
Io voglio provar	160	
Navicella che ten vai	165	
Io mi parto	169	*ib.*
Pera Clori	176	
Cruda Lilla	183	
Mi voglio far intendere	187	5055
Voi vene pentirete	198	5056

Oblong Quarto. Early part of the xviiith cent. [*Add. Mss.* 5331.]

196.

Duetts, for two trebles, composed by Agostino Steffani, towards the end of the seventeenth century.

Vuol il ciel	p. 1	
Che sarà di qual pensiero	7	
Parlo e rido	20	
Troppo cruda	24	Another copy in *Add. Ms.* 5056
Quando un Eroe	36	*ib.*
O care catene	48	*ib.*
Porto ne lumi	53	*ib.*
Nò nò non voglio	60	*ib.*
Tienmi il cor	66	*ib.*
O mia vita	70	
Su ferisci	75	5055
Ribellatevi	85	*ib.*
Pria che faccia	93	*ib.*
Saldi marmi	104	5056
Ravvediti, mio core	124	*ib.*
Se a morire	132	
Quanto care	138	5055
Cangia pensier	151	*ib.*
Hò scherzato	160	*ib.*
Soavissime catene	171	*ib.*

Oblong Quarto. Early part of the xviiith cent. [*Add. Mss.* 5332.]

197.

A volume, containing the following compositions, by Henry Purcell.

The Music in the Opera of "King Arthur." Full score. Incomplete. fol. 1.

The Music in "The Libertine." Full score. Incomplete. fol. 54.

An Ode set to Music for the Yorkshire Feast. Full score. fol. 59.

This volume bears, at the commencement, the autograph signatures of Dr. William Croft, organist of Westminster Abbey, and of James Kent, organist of Winchester Cathedral.

Folio. End of the xviith cent. [*Add. Mss.* 5333.]

198.

"Sylla," an Opera, by Giovanni Buononcini. Quarto. Middle of the xviiith cent. [*Add. Mss.* 5334.]

199.

A volume of Duetts for different voices, by Italian composers of the seventeenth century.

*Piaggie fiorite. (Pietro Torri.) p. 1		Pria ch'adori (H. Barnabei.) p. 128		
*Per te, mio bene. (id.) . . . 15		Prendi amor. (Ant. Veracini.) 146		
*Dall' arco. (id.) 25		*M'incatenò cupido. (Fr. Ant.		
*Odi, O Lilla. (id.) 30		Pistocchi.) 173		
*Da me lungi. (id.) 46		*D'improviso rieda. (Feroci.) . 178		
*Valli secrete. (id.) 63		Amor, che far deggio. (id.) . 181		
*Vivo in pene. (id.) 69		*Che sarà di te. (id.) . . . 189		
Sol di pianto. (id.) 74		Aure care. (id.) 194		
*Chi dirà. (A. Stradella.) . . 96		Nel seno d'amore. (id.) . . 299		
*Troppo grave. (id.) 119		Dal mio sen. (id.) 213		

The pieces marked thus * are also in *Add. Ms.* 5056.

Oblong Quarto. Early part of the xviiith cent. [*Add. Mss.* 5335.]

200.

A volume containing Rounds, Catches, Madrigals, etc., in score, chiefly taken from the three works edited by Thomas Ravenscroft, at the beginning of the 17th century, intitled Pammelia, Deuteromelia, and Melismata. At the end are twelve organ voluntaries, by Dr. William Croft.

Trole the bowl	(Pammelia.) . . . . fol. 1
Farewell, mine own sweet heart . . .	(id.) . . . . . . ib.
Stir the fire	 2
Brooms for old shoes	(Melismata.) 3
My mistress will not be content	(id.) . . . . . . ib.

Oblong Folio. Latter part of the xviiith cent. [*Add. Mss.* 5336.]

201.

A volume containing
The Music in "Timon of Athens," in score, by Henry Purcell. p. 1.
The Music in "Bonduca," in score, by Henry Purcell. p. 48.
"Clori, son fido amante." A Madrigal for five voices, by Alessandro Stradella. p. 80.
"Thou soft invader," a Duett, in score, from Solomon, by Dr. William Boyce. p. 94.
Six Sonatas for a violin and bass, by — Graff. p. 108.
Two Songs, in four parts, by Le Tessier, 1597. Begin. "Au joly bois," and "Su la riva." p. 148.
"Round about"; a four part Song, by John Bennett. (From Ravenscroft's *Brief Discourse.*) p. 152.
"Jack boy, ho boy"; a round from Pammelia. p. 153.
"Sing we this roundelay"; round for four voices. p. 154.
"Here, drawer"; catch for three voices. p. 154.
A Glee in praise of Sack, by Dr. John Wilson. p. 156.
"View here the youth"; an elegy for three voices, by Dr. William Boyce. p. 160.
Folio. xviiith cent. [*Add. Mss.* 5337.]

202.

The Psalms of David [the commencement only of each], set to music as Canons, and dedicated to King James I., by Sydrach Rahel. Quarto. Beginning of the xviith cent. It formerly belonged to the Old Royal Library. [*Add. Mss.* 5341.]

203.

A volume of antient English Songs, for two, three, and four voices, by different composers, of the latter part of the fifteenth and beginning of the sixteenth centuries.

The farther I go, the more behynde. Two voices. (Wm. Newark.) fol. 4 b.
A! my harte, I knowe you well. Two voices 5
What causyth me wofull thoughtis. Two voices. (Wm. Newark.) . 6 b.
So far, I trow, from remedy. Two voices. (id.) . . . . 8 b.
My wofull hart in paynfule werynees. Two voices. (Sheryngam.) . . 9 b.
Printed in Burney's *History of Music*, vol. ii. p. 544.

This volume belonged to Dr. Robert Fayrfax, by whom
some of the music is composed; and subsequently to Ralph

Thoresby, of Leeds.   An account is given of it by Dr. Burney, and Sir J. Hawkins, in their Histories of Music.
   Vellum.   Quarto.   End of the xvth cent.   [*Add. Mss.*
5465.]

204.

A collection of Latin and English Hymns and Songs, in parts,
composed towards the end of the fifteenth century.   Some
of them have been printed by Joseph Ritson, in his *Antient
Songs*, 8vo, 1790.

Jhesus autem hodie regressus est . . . } *Epiphanie* . . . . . fol. 37 *b.*
When Jhesus Criste baptyzed was . . }

At the end are the following mottos, " Hyt ys gode to be gracius, sayde John
Trouluffe." " Welle fare thyn herte, sayde Smert."

Clangat tuba, martir Thome . . . } *Sancti Thome* . . . . . 38 *b.*
Oute of the chaffe was pured this corne }

Man, asay, and axe mercy . . . . 39 *b.*
Jhesu, fili Virginis . . . . . . } *De Nativitate* . . . . 40 *b.*
Jhesu, of a mayde thou woldest be borne }
Jhesu, for thy mercy endelesse . . . . 41 *b.*
The beste songe, as hit semeth me . . . . 42 *b.*
To many a wille have Y go . . . . 43 *b.*
Salve, regina misereoordie . . . . 44 *b.*
Pray for us, thou Prince of pes. *De Sancto Johanne* . . . . . 45 *b.*
O blessed Lord, fulle of pete . . . . 46 *b.*
The beste rede that I can . . . . 47 *b.*
For alle Cristen saulys pray we. *In fine Nativitatis* . . . . 48 *h.*
Blessed mote thou be, swete Jhesus. *De Nativitate.* (Smert.) . . 49 *b.*
Y have been a foster long and meney day. Imperfect . . . . . 50 *h.*
Nesciens mater. Alleluya. (Trouluffe.) . . . . 51 *b.*
Beati Dei genitrix. (Ric. Mowere.) . . . . 52 *b.*
Nesciens mater Virgo. (Trouluffe.) . . . . 53 *b.*
Id. (Trouluffe. Smert.) . . . . 54 *b.*
Ave, regina celorum . . . . 55 *b.*
Regina celi, letare. (Ric. Mower.) . . . . 56 *b.*
O lux beata Trinitas . . . . 57 *b.*
Te mane laudum carmine . . . . 58 *b.*
Lumen ad revelacionem. (Syr T. Packe.) . . . . 59 *b.*
Secundum verbum tuum. (*id.*) . . . . 60 *b.*
Stella celi extirpavit. (Syr W. Hawte, Miles.) . . . . 61 *b.*
My wofulle hert of alle gladnesse bareyne . . . . 62 *b.*
Be pes, ʒe make me spille my ale . . . . 63 *b.*
Absens of ʒeu causeth me to syghe . . . . 64 *b.*
The hye desire that Y have for to se . . . . 65 *b.*
O blessed Lord, how may this be . . . . 66 *b.*
Thow man enured with temptacione . . . . 67 *b.*
Now, helpe, fortune, of thy godenesse . . . . 68 *b.*
Fayre and discrete . . . . 69 *b.*
Rex summe. A Mass. (Thomas Packe.) . . . . 70 *b.*
Gaudete in Domino. Missa pro hominibus 12 notis cumpas. (*id.*). . 81 *b.*
Te Deum laudamus. We prayse the, almysty God. Verse and chorus.
(Syr Thos. Packe.) . . . . fol. 92 *b.*
Festa dies . . . . 103 *b.*
Gaude, Virgo Mater. 12 notis cumpas . . . . 104 *b.*
Kyrye eleyson. Et in terra pax. Qui tollis. (Edmund Sturges.) . . 106 *b.*
Gaude, Sancta Magdalena. (Syr Thos. Packe.) . . . . . . 109 *b.*
Et in terrâ pax. A Mass. (Henricus Petyre.) . . . . 110 *b.*
Dicant nunc Judei. (Joh. Cornysche.) . . . . 117 *b.*
Benedicamus Domino . . . . 118 *b.*
Salve, festa dies 119
Maria Virgo, intercede . . . . 119 *b.*
Nesciens mater. *Ad festum nativitatis Domini* . . . . . . 120 *b.*
Salve, regina. (W. P.) . . . . 121 *b.*
Anima mea liquefacta est. (W. P.) . . . . 126 *b.*
Nunc, Jhesu, te petimus . . . . 128 *b.*
Alone, alone, mournyng . . . . 130 *b.*
My herte ys in grete mornyng . . . . 132 *b.*
Passetyme with goode company *The Kynges Balade* 133 *b.* and 138 *b.*
So put yn fere I dare not speke . . . . 134 *b.*

Vellum and paper. Quarto. End of the xvth and beginning
of the xvith cent. [*Add. Mss.* 5665.]

205.

Fragments of single voice parts of old English Songs, very
roughly noted. See Ritson's *Ancient Songs*, 1790, pp.
xxxviii. xl.

Duodecimo. xvth cent. [*Add. Mss.* 5666.]

206.

"Traité de l'harmonie des sons et de leurs rapports, ou la Musique theorique et pratique ancienne et moderne examinée dès
son origine, par Le P. D. Charles Hebert, D. Q. R. M^{re}. D.
S. H^{me}. Lecteur honoraire de Philosophie dans l'Université de
Boulogne, l'an 1733." Quarto. [*Add. Mss.* 6137.]

207.

"Recueil de Chansons, avec accompagnemens de deux violons,
basson ou quinte, et basse continue," by Jean Jacques Rousseau. In the handwriting of the composer. Oblong Quarto.
Latter part of the xviiith cent. [*Add. Mss.* 6145.]

208.

"Airs de Jean Jacques Rousseau," with accompaniments for
two violins, tenor and bass. In the handwriting of the composer, and dedicated to La Comtesse d'Egmont. 4 Vols.
Quarto. Latter part of the xviiith cent. [*Add. Mss.* 6146-
6149.]

209.

Latin Treatises on Music: *Tunstede & others*

" Quatuor principalia tocius artis musice." The prologue begins, " Quemadmodum inter triticum et zizamina.", The *fol. 4.* work begins, " Quoniam circa musicam, Deo auxiliante." fol. 7. b.

This Treatise has been erroneously ascribed to Thomas of Tewksbury by Anthony Wood, and to John Hamboys [Hanboys] by Bishop Tanner. There appears little doubt, for the reasons assigned by Dr. Burney, in his *History of Music*, vol. ii. p. 395, that it was written by Simon Tunstede, A.D. 1351.

" Musica Magistri Franconis, cum addicionibus et opinionibus diversorum." The prologue begins, " Cum de plana musica quidam." The first chapter, " Mensurabilis musica est cantus." fol. 64 *b*.

The treatise of Franco is printed by Gerbertus, *Script. Eccles. de Musica*, vol. iii. p. i.

This Treatise appears to be a commentary upon the writings of Franco, by John Hanboys, who flourished about the year 1470. It concludes thus, " Explicit Summa Magistri Johannis Hanboys, Doctoris Musice reverendi, super musicam continuam et discretam."

Vellum. Quarto. xvth cent. [*Add. Mss.* 8866.]

210.

Sacred Music, by Henry Purcell, in the handwriting of Vincent Novello; being the Anthems, Latin Psalms, Canons, Church Services, Hymns, and Sacred Songs published by the latter under the title of " Purcell's Sacred Music." 7 Vols. Oblong Folio. Written in 1829-1832. [*Add. Mss.* 9071-9077.]

211.

" Nor can I think my suit is vain;" a song and chorus, in full score, composed by, and in the autograph of Joseph Haydn, in the year 1794, at the desire of the Earl of Abingdon, and by him given to T. Monzani, the celebrated flute player, who in 1821 presented it to the British Museum.

Mr. Monzani states, that it was intended to form part of an oratorio, but that Haydn never did more towards its completion.

The poetry is taken from the introductory stanzas prefixed to Nedham's translation of Selden's " Mare Clausum," fol. 1652.

Oblong Quarto. [*Add. Mss.* 9284.]

212.

11th Century

Latin Treatises on Music :

The " Micrologus" of Guido Aretinus, wanting the commencement of the " Prologus." fol. 1.

Printed by Gerbertus, *Script. Eccles. de Musica*, vol. ii. p. 1. See also *Harl. Ms.* 281; *Arundel. Ms.* 339; *Add. Ms.* 4915.

Epistle of Guido Aretinus, " de ignoto cantu," addressed " Beatissimo atque dulcissimo Fratri M." fol. 11.

Printed by Gerbertus, *ib.* vol. ii. p. 43. See also *Harl. Ms.* 281, and *Arundel Ms.* 339.

The Enchiridion of Oddo, Abbot of Cluny, in Burgundy, who lived in the tenth century, in form of a dialogue. The prologue begins, " Petistis obnixe." The work begins, " Quid est musica ?" fol. 15 *b*.

Printed by Gerbertus, *ib.* vol. i. p. 251. See also *Harl. Ms.* 281, and *Add. Ms.* 4915.

Formulæ for singing in the eight Ecclesiastical Tones. fol. 23.

Vellum. Quarto. xiith cent. [*Add. Mss.* 10,335.]

213.

Treatises on Music : *Tucke's Ms.*

A Treatise, beginning, " Quilibet in arte practica mensurabilis cantus." fol. 6.

It concludes at fol. 18, and is subscribed " Qd. Dunstable." and is, probably, the treatise by John Dunstable, mentioned in Burney, vol. ii. p. 399, and Hawkins, vol. ii. p. 298.

A Treatise or collections on musical figures, numbers, and proportions. Begin. " Imprimis loquamur de typo." fol. 18 *b*.

At ff. 23 *b*., 39, and 64 *b*., occurs the name of " Joannes Tucke," and at the end, fol. 73 *b*., is written, " Proporciones secundum Joannem Otteby, Magistrum in Musica, expliciunt feliciter, vicesimo sexto die Marcii, 1500. Script. per me, Dnm. Joannem Tucke, in Artibus Bacchalaurium, necnon hujus artis non inexpertum."

Excerpts relative to musical proportions by colors. (See *Lansdowne Ms.* 763. fol. 87 *b*.); also excerpts from Guido's Micrologus, etc. fol. 97 *b*.

At the end is written, " La fine qd. Dns. Joannes Tucke, socius quondam perpetuus Novi Collegii Beate Marie Wyntonie in Oxonio, ac in Artibus Baccalaureus." It would therefore appear that Tucke was only the transcriber of the volume.

Small Quarto. [*Add. Mss.* 10,336.]

214.

" Elizabeth Rogers, her Virginall book," containing the following pieces of vocal and instrumental music.

Folio. Written about A.D. 1656. [*Add. Mss.* 10,337.]

215.

A volume, apparently in the composer's handwriting, the contents of which are as follows:—

In the midst of life. Four voices. (" Made in the tyme of my sicknes,
   Oct. 1657.") . . . . fol. 169 b.
O Domine Deus. Four voices . . . . 165 b.
Turne thou us, O good Lord. Four voices. (Dated 1655.) 172
Turne thee againe. Four voices 177
Quid comisisti, Jesu. Four voices 181
Ego sum panis. Four voices 183
Jubilate Deo. Four voices 187
Amor Jesu, dulcis amor. Four voices . . . . 190 b.
O bone Jesu. Four voices 193
Audite, coeli, audite. Four voices . . . . 196 b.
Jesu dulcedo cordium. Four voices . . . . 199 b.
Te Deum laudamus. Four voices. (Dated 1649.) 204
Gloria Patri. Four voices . . . . 215 b.
O quam jucundum. Four voices. (Dated 1651.) 217
Gloria Patri, qui creavit nos. Four voices. (Dated 1651.) . . . . 221 b.
Glory be to God on high. Four voices . . . . 223 b.
Sanctus and Gloria. Four voices . . . . - 226
Gloria in excelsis. Five voices 228
Bone Jesu, verbum Patris. Five voices . . . . 230 b.
Harke, sheaphard swaynes. Five voices. (For the Nativity.) . . . 234 b.
Bussie tyme. Five voices. (For the B. Innocents day.) 239
Brightest of dayes. Five voices. (For the Epiphany.) . . . . . 242 b.
Whisper it easily. Five voices. (On the Passion of our B. Saviour.) 246 b.
Ryse, hart, thy Lord. Five voices. (For the Resurrection.) . . . 250 b.
Looke upp, all eyes. Five voices. (For the Ascension.) . . . . . 255 b.
The Lord in thy adversity. Five voices . . . . 259 b.
Hosanna filio David. Six voices . . . . 266 b.
A musick strange. Five voices. (For Whitsunday. Dated 1669.) . 270 b.

Folio. Written between 1631 and 1669. [*Add. Mss.* 10,338.]

216.

A volume, containing

Dance tunes, Nos. 1 to 26. Treble and Bass parts only.
It is not stated whether originally written for a greater number of instruments.

No.		No.	
1. The two merry Lasses.	fol. 2	14. Gibbons, his Allmaine .	fol. 6
2. The merry young Man	. 2 b.	15. Mainard's Allmaine	. ib.
3. The merry Batchelor .	. ib.	16. Douland's Allmaine	. 6 b.
4. The humming Batchelor .	3	17. An Allmaine . . .	. ib.
5. The merry Clerke . .	. 3 b.	18. Id.	. 7
6. The merry old Woman	. ib.	19. Ca me, ca thee . . .	. ib.
7. The merry old Man .	. 4	20. An Allmaine	. 7 b.
8. The Battel of Harloe .	. 4 b.	21. Stephen Thomas, his Al-	
9. The Bee	. ib.	maine	. ib.
10. Robart's Almaine . :	. 5	22. An Allmaine	. 8
11. The Silver Swanne . .	. ib.	23. Id.	. 8 b.
(Taken from O. Gibbons's		24. Bull's Toye	. ib.
Madrigal of that name.)		25. Stephen Thomas, his 2	
12. Bateman's Allmaine .	. 5 b.	Allmaine	. 9
13. Lake's Allmaine . .	. ib.	26. An Almaine	. ib.

Masques and Dance Tunes. Treble and Bass only. Nos.
1 to 38.

No.		No.	
1. The Queene's first Masque. f. 10 b.		2. The Queene's second Masque. f. 11 b.	

M

No.

110. Williams his Love . . fol. 47
111. Waters his Love . . . 47 b.
112. Broxboorn-berry Masque. ib.
113. The New Yeares Gift . . 48
114. Bateman's Masque . . . 48 b.
115. Squier's Masque . . . ib.
116. The first of the Temple . 49
117. The second 49
118. The third . . . . . 49 b.
119. The first of Sir J. Pag-
        ginton's . . . . . ib.
120. The second 50
121. The third . . . . 50 b.
122. The first of the Temple
        Anticke . . . . . ib.
123. The second 51
124. The first of the Temple
        Masques . . . . . ib.

No.

125. The second . . . . . fol. 51 b.
126. The third . . . . . ib.
127. The first of the Prince, his
        Masque . . . . . ib.
128. The second 52
129. The third . . . . . ib.
130. Lincolnes Inne Masque . 52 b.
131. The Prince, his Masque . ib.
132. The Apes' Dance at the
        Temple 53
133. Grayes Inne Masque . . 53 b. —
134. Id. . . . . ib. —
135. The first of the Prince, his
        Masque 54
136. The second . . . . . ib.
137. }
138. } Anonymous . . . . 54 b.

Thirty-nine Fantasies, Airs, Corants, and Pavans, in two parts,
Treble and Bass, by Matthew Locke.   fol. 105.

" Matthew Locke, his little Consort of three parts, 1656." A-
printed copy of the Treble and Tenor parts only.   fol. 130.

    Oblong Quarto.   Middle of the xviith cent.   [Add. Mss.
10,444.]

217.

A volume, containing:

The " Royall Consort," by William Lawes.   In three parts.
Imperfect.   fol. 1.

    Airs, by William Lawes.   Violin and bass.   ff. 40 and
69 b.

    Airs, by John Jenkins.   Violin and bass.   ff. 57 b. and
85 b.

    Airs, Fancies, etc., by M. Locke.   Violin and bass.   ff.
62 b. and 89.

    Airs, by J. Coperario.   Two bass parts.   ff. 95 b. and
117.

    " Thus Cupid commences his rapes."   Song.   Anonymous.
fol. 103 b.

    " Depuis que j'ayme."   Song.   Anonymous.   fol. 104 b.

    " Le Ballet du Roy, 1671, de Psyche," by Baptiste [Lully].
Violin and bass.   ff. 105 b. and 124 b.

    " Le Ballet de 1670," by Baptiste [Lully].   Violin and
bass.   ff. 111 b. and 131 b.

    The music of these ballets should consist of four parts.

    Oblong Quarto.   Latter part of the xviith cent.   [Add. Mss.
10,445.]

218.

A Register of Performances, with names of the singers, etc., at the Opera House in the Haymarket, by Francis Colman, British Consul at Leghorn, and father of George Colman, the dramatic writer; from 1712 to 1734. Small Quarto. [*Add. Mss.* 11,258.]

219.

" Judith," an Oratorio,' in three acts. Full score. In the hand-writing of the composer, Dr. Thomas Augustine Arne. 3 Vols. Oblong Quarto. Middle of the xviiith cent. [*Add. Mss.* 11,515–11,517.]

220.

" Comus," a Masque. The poetry by John Milton, set to music by Dr. Thomas Augustine Arne. Full score.

At fol. 59 are introduced two printed songs, and a chorus, from " L'Allegro ed il Pensieroso " of Handel; and prefixed are five songs, set to music by Henry Lawes, as performed at Ludlow Castle, Oct. 1634.

Quarto. Middle of the xviiith cent. [*Add. Mss.* 11,518.]

The eleven following volumes, in the handwriting of Dr. Charles Burney, consist of Musical Extracts made by him, many of which are inserted as illustrations and specimens in his *History of Music*, 1776.'

221.

Volume I. of Dr. Burney's Musical Extracts, containing:

Double Chant, sung at St. Paul's church, Oct. 20, 1780 . . . . fol. 2
Exempla (Discant.) quatuor vocum. (Froschius, 1535.) . . . . . 2 b.
Fuga ad minimam. (Jodocus Pratensis [Josquin des Pres], 1547, ex Glareano.) 4
Tablature of the Lute, from Thos. Mace's *Musical Monument*, p. 84 . 6 b.
Lessons from Morris's Welsh Musical Mss. . . . . 8 b.
Lord, who shall dwell in thy tabernacle. (Anthem for five voices, by Robert White, 1581.) . . . . 9 b.
" Non nobis Domine." (Canon for three voices, ascribed to Wm. Byrd.) . . . . 12 b.
" Hey down, down, sing ye now after me." A Round of four voices to the plain song . . . . : 14

M 2

Quarto. Latter part of the xviiith cent. [*Add. Mss.* 11,581.]

222.

Volume II. of Dr. Burney's Musical Extracts, containing:

Quarto. Latter part of the XVIIIth cent. [*Add. Mss.* 11,582.]

223.

Volume III. of Dr. Burney's Musical Extracts, containing:

" Præter rerum seriem." Motett for seven voices. " Dalla musica
  nova di Adriano [Willaert] " . . . . 14 *b.*
" Inviolata, integra, et casta es." Motett for seven voices. By the same. 20 *b.*
" Ogni loco mi porgi doglia." Madrigal for five voices, by Gianetto da
  Palestrina. " Dal primo libro de le Muse." Venice, 1550 . . . 27 *b.*
" Sound out, my voice." Madrigal for five voices, by Gianetto da Palestrina. An English adaptation from the original, intitled " Ves-
  tiva i colli," and published by Nich. Yonge, in the *Musica Trans-
  alpina*, Book 1. 1588 . . . . 29 *b.*

" Formoso vermi."　Epithalamium for five voices.　Jachet Berchem.
　" Ex lib. l^{mo} Cipriani [de Rore], cum quibusdam aliis motetorum."
　1544 . . . . fol. 31
" Invidioso amor."　Madrigal for five voices.　Aless°. Striggio.　" Dal
　2da libro de le Muse, composto da diversi Musici."　1559 . . . . 33 *b.*
" Sans lever le pied."　Chanson à 5.　(J. Clemens non Papa.) . . . 35 *b.*
" Adieu celle que j'ay servi."　Chanson à 5.　(Gerardus [Dyricke ?]) . 36 *b.*
　See the same words, *App.* to *Royal Mss.* 23–25, but the music is
　different.
" La belle Marguerite."　Chanson à 5.　(J. Clemens non Papa.) . . 37 *b.*
" Susanne un jour."　Chanson à 5.　(Orlando di Lasso.) . . . . . 38 *b.*

Oblong Quarto.　Latter part of the XVIIIth cent.　[*Add. Mss.*
11,583.]

224.

Volume IV. of Dr. Burney's Musical Extracts, containing :

" Queste non son più lagrime." Chanson à 4.	Orlando di Lasso.	fol. 2 *b.*	Printed 1555
" Sto core mio."　Chanson à 4.	. . id.	. . . 3	. . . —
" Tu traditora."　Chanson à 4.	. . id.	. . . 3 *b.*	. . . —
" En espoir vis."　Chanson à 4.	. . id.	. . . 4	. . . —
" Alma nimis."　Chanson à 4.	. . id.	. . . 4 *b.*	. . . —
" Calami sonum ferentes." Chanson à 4.	Cipriano di Rore	. . 5 *b.*	
" Madonne, l'arte nostra." Canzona à 4	Perissone Cambio	. . 7	. . . 1551
" Vi voglio dire, donne." Canzona à 4	. . id.	. . . 7 *b.*	. . . —
" Chi la gagliarda." Canzona à 4.	Baldassara Donato.	. 8	. . . 1555
" Te parlo, tu me ridi." Canzona à 4	. . id.	. . . 8 *b.*	. . . —
" Da pacem, Domine." Motett, 4 voices	Adrian Willaert	. . 9	. . . 1563
" Veni creator."　Canon, 3 voices.	Giuseppe Zarlino	. . 9 *b.*	. . . 1573
" Deposuit potentes." From a Magnificat	G. P. A. da Palestrina.	10	
" Domine, quid multiplicati sunt." Motett, 4 voices	Claude Goudimel	. 10 *b.*	. . . 1554
" Ave, Maria." Motett, 3 voices.	Claude le Jeune, or Claude Goudimel.	13	. . . 1549
" Cessez, mes yeux." Chanson à 4.	Thomas Crequillon	. 13 *b.*	. . . 1555
" Cessez, mes yeux." (Réponse.) Chanson à 4.	Jean Louys .	. . . 14	. . . —
" Donnes secours." Chanson à 4.	Petit Jean de Latre	. 15 *b.*	. . . —
" Vivons joyeusement." Chanson à 4	Morel	. . . . 16 *b.*	. . . —
" Fille qui prend." Chanson à 4.	John Crespel	. . 17 *b.*	. . . —
" Misericorde."　Chanson à 4	Clemens non Papa	. 18 *b.*	. . . —
" Puisque voules." Chanson à 4.	. . id.	. . . 19 *b.*	. . . —
" Avant mes jours." Chanson à 4.	Claude le Jeune	. 20 *b.*	. . . 1559
" Si par fortune." Chanson à 4.	Geraert Hobrecht	. 21 *b.*	. . . —
" Toutes les nuyctz." Chanson à 4	Josquin Baston	. 23 *b.*	. . . —

" Bon jour, ma mie." Chanson à 4.	Claude le Jeune	. fol. 24 b.	Printed 1559
" Le feu qui m'ard." Chanson à 4.	id.	. 25 b.	—
" Puis qu'il convient." Chanson à 4	Petrus Heylanus	. 26 b.	—
" Par trop aymer." Chanson à 4.	Pier. Manchicourt.	. 27 b.	—
" Sans liberte." Chanson à 4	Jan. Gerard	. 28 b.	—
A Canon without words. 3 voices.	Joh. Okenheim.	. 29 b.	
" Domine Deus." Motett, 3 voices.	Crist. Morales	. 30	. 1549
" Heu mihi, Domine." Motett, 4 voices	Jac. Clemens non Papa. 30 b.		. 1553
" O lux et decus." Motett, 4 voices.	id.	. 32 b.	—
" Adjuro vos." Motett, 4 voices.	id.	. 34	—
" Pater noster." Motett, 4 voices.	Philippe de Wildre	. 35 b.	—
" Congratulamini mihi." Motett, 4 voices	Claude le Jeune, or Claude Goudimel.	36 b.	. 1539
" Puer natus est." Motett, 3 voices	Crist. Morales	. 37 b.	. 1543
" Quam pulchra es." Motett, 3 voices	Const. Festa	. 38 b.	—
" Sancta Maria." Motett, 3 voices.	id.	. 39 b.	—
" O lux beatissima." Motett, 6 voices	Adrian Willaert	. 40 b.	. 1558
" I vidi in terra." Madrigal, 6 voices	id.	. 42 b.	. 1559
" Regi regis regum arcana cano." Canon, 3 voices	Henry Lawes	. 44 b.	. 1650
" Aspice, Domine." Motett, 6 voices	Adrian Willaert	. 45	. 1559
" Liet'e seren' in vista." Madrigal, 4 voices	Jacques Arcadelt	. 46 b.	. 1541
" Quando ritrovo." Madrigal, 4 voices	Const. Festa	. 47	—
" Cosi soave el fuoco." Madrigal, 4 voices	id.	. 47 b.	—

Oblong Quarto. Latter part of the xviiith cent. [*Add.
Mss.* 11,584.]

225.

Volume V. of Dr. C. Burney's Musical Extracts, containing:

" Chi prend'amor à gioco." Madrigal, three voices, upon a ground Base, with accompaniments for two violins. (Tarquinio Merula.)	Printed 1635	f. 2
" Con nobil arte." Aria a voce sola. (id.)		4 b.
" Nominativo hic." Four voices. (id.)		5
" Nominativo quis." Four voices. (id.)		8 b.
" Rose beate." Madrigal, two voices. (Aless°. Grandi.)	1626	12
Fragments of Italian Melody in the seventeenth century, from the works of Pallavicino, Cifra, Merula, and Facho		12 b.
" Dormivo, e mi bacciasti." Madrigal, two voices. (Giov. Ferrari.)	1628	15
" Noel, noel." Four voices. (Eustache du Caurroy.)	1610	17
" Noel, noel." Four voices. (id.)	—	17 b.

Oblong Quarto. Latter part of the XVIIIth cent. [*Add.
Mss.* 11,585.]

226.

Volume VI. of Dr. C. Burney's Musical Extracts, containing:

Extracts from " Per arma justitie." Mass. Five voices. (John Marbeck.). . . . . fol. 17 *b.*

Extracts from " Albanus." Mass. Five voices. (Dr. Rob. Fayrfax.) 20 *b.*

" Gloria." From a Mass. Three voices. (*id.*) . . . . 25 *b.*

Extracts from " O Michael." Mass. Three and four voices. (John Taverner.) . . . . *ib.*

" From depth of sinne." Motett. Three voices. (Will. Byrd.) . 27 *b.*
    (From *Songs of sundrie Natures*, 1589.)

" Rejoyce with hart," (from the same.) Motett. Four voices. (*id.*) . 28 *b.*

" In nomine," without words. Motett. Five voices. (Dr. John Bull.) 29 *b.*

" Precamur, sancte Domine." Motett. Five voices. (Robert White.) 31

" In nomine." Motett. Five voices. (*id.*) . . . . 32 *b.*

" With wreathes of rose." Madrigal. Five voices. (W. Cobbold.) . 34
    (From the *Triumphs of Oriana*, 1601.)

" O, had I wings." Motett. Five voices. (John Milton.) . . . . 34 *b.*
    (From the *Teares and Lamentacions of a Sorrowful Soule*, 1614.)

" Deare, when to thee." Song. One voice. (Alfonso Ferabosco, Jun.) 37

" So, so, leave off." Song. One voice. (*id.*) . . . . 37 *b.*

" Hence, stars." Madrigal. Five voices. (Michael Este.) 38
    (From the *Triumphs of Oriana*, 1601.)

" All creatures now," (from the same.) Madrigal. Five voices. (John Bennet.) . . . . 39 *b.*

A " Fancy," in five parts. From the L'Estrange collection. (John Ward) . . . . 41 *b.*

" Where fancy fond." Madrigal. Five voices. (Will. Byrd.) . . . 43 *b.*
    (From *Psalmes, Sonnets, and Songs of Sadness and Pietie*, 1588.)

Specimens of Dr. Blow's crudities. 45

" Since the spring comes on." Pastoral ballad. (Dr. John Blow.) . . 47
    (From the 4th book of the *Theatre of Musick*.)

Fragments of three Ballads from the *Amphion Anglicus*. (*id.*) . . . *ib.*

Oblong Quarto. Latter part of the XVIIIth cent. [*Add. Mss.* 11,586.]

227.

Volume VII. of Dr. Charles Burney's Musical Extracts, containing :

Extracts from a Mass, " Gloria tibi Trinitas." Six voices. (John Taverner.) . . . . fol. 2

" Euge, bone," a Mass, for six voices. (Christopher Tye.) . . . . . 7 *b.*
    (Some parts which were wanting in the old copies, have been supplied by Dr. Burney.)

" O tu, qui dans oracula." A two part song, from the prologue to a work intitled " A new discourse of a stale subject, called the Metamorphosis of AJAX," written by Sir John Harrington, under the name of Misacmos, 1596 . . . . 17 *b.*
    In the " Nugæ Antiquæ," Sir John Harrington states that the tune was composed by his father, and that it used to be sung by K. Henry the Eighth, " in pleasaunte moode," and was called the *Black Sauntus*, or Monke's Hymne to Saunte Satane, made when King Henry had spoyld their singing. The music given by Dr. Burney agrees with the printed copy of the original work, but differs from that in the appendix to Sir J. Hawkins's *History of Music*, which is a Canon, in three parts.

The 100th Psalm, with parts by Dr. [John] Dowland, from Ravenscroft's *Psalms*, 2d Edition, 1633 18

The 134th Psalm, in four parts, by Claude le Jeune . . . . *ib.*

N

Oblong Quarto. Latter part of the xviiith cent. [*Add.
Mss*. 11,587.]

228.

Volume VIII. of Dr. Charles Burney's Musical Extracts, containing:

Quarto. Latter part of the XVIIIth cent. [*Add. Mss.* 11,588.]

229.

Volume IX. of Dr. Charles Burney's Musical Extracts, containing:

An Index in Notation of the 5th and 6th volumes of Dr. Tudway's Church Music, in the *Harl. Mss.* 7341-2, with a general alphabetical Index of the composers' names . . . . fol. 2

Chants or Chorales from the Studij di Palestrina, by G. M. Nanino, B. Nanino, F. Anerio, A. Cifra, B. Giovanelli, O. Benevoli, P. L. Palestrina, Rubino, Tomasso, G. Todi, Magiorana, Josquin des Pres, and Marcello Tortora . . . . 19 b.

" Regole del contrappunto pratico di Nicola Sala." Printed at Naples, 1794. Book 1 and part of Book 2 25

Oblong Quarto. Latter part of the XVIIIth cent. [*Add. Mss.* 11,589.]

230.

Volume X. of Dr. Charles Burney's Musical Extracts, containing:

The remainder of Book 2. of the " Regole del contrappunto di Nicola Sala ; " continued from the preceding volume.

Oblong Quarto. Latter part of the XVIIIth cent. [*Add. Mss.* 11,590.]

231.

Volume XI. of Dr. Charles Burney's Musical Extracts, containing:

Oblong Quarto. Latter part of the xviiith cent. [*Add. Mss.*
11,591.]

232.

A volume of Songs, Canons, Dialogues, Catches, and Rounds,
composed about the middle of the seventeenth century.

Folio. Middle of the xviiith cent. [*Add. Mss.* 11,608.]

233.

A Latin Gradual, with musical notes, probably written for the use of some church in Germany. It is imperfect at the end. Vellum. Folio. xith cent. [*Add. Mss.* 11,669.]

234.

Twelve Letters from Dr. Crotch, Samuel Wesley, R. J. S. Stevens, etc., to Vincent Novello, relative to the works of Purcell, 1828-1830. Presented by V. Novello, 12th May, 1840. Quarto. [*Add. Mss.* 11,731.]

235.

Orders, Minutes, etc., of the "Academy of Vocal Musick," [generally called the "Academy of Ancient Music,"] from the 7th Jan. 172⅔, to the 26th May, 1731. Presented by Vincent Novello, 1 June, 1840. Folio. [*Add. Mss.* 11,732.]

236.

Latin Hymns and Offices for the whole year. Imperfect at the beginning and end. Vellum. Quarto. XIIIth cent. [*Add. Mss.* 12,194.]

237.

The Music in " Macbeth," with the names of the Singers, viz., Lee, Spalding, Courco, Bowman, Mrs. Willis, and Mrs. Hodgson. Bowman or Boman came on the stage as a boy about the year 1673, and sang a man's part in Lee's Tragody of " Theodosius " in 1680; but as the names of the females do not appear amongst the Dramatis Personæ till 1696, that year may be assumed as the probable date of the Manuscript. Lee, Bowman, Mrs. Willis, and Mrs. Hodgson sang together in the " Loves of Mars and Venus," composed by John Eccles and Godfrey Finger, 1697; Courco and Spalding sang Eccles's Duett, " Wine does Wonders," in " The Morose Reformer," about the same period, and all their names appear to many of the detached songs, engraved by Thomas Cross, in the latter part of the seventeenth and beginning of the eighteenth century.

There is extant another copy, corresponding in every respect with this Manuscript, [*see* " Shakspeare's Songs by William Linley," and also the preface to Vincent Novello's edition of Purcell's Works,] and bearing the name of John Eccles, who began to attain celebrity as a dramatic composer between the years 1690 and 1700. The music, although in some parts strikingly similar to that attributed by tradition to Matthew Locke, (of which it is believed no manuscript or printed copy exists, earlier than that published by Dr. Boyce towards the latter part of the eighteenth century,) is not sufficiently identical to warrant the charge of actual plagiarism.

With the exception of the two lines beginning " Hark, I'm cali'd," which are by Shakspere, the words are from Sir W. D'Avenant's adaptation of the Tragedy published 1674, and are partly taken from Middleton's Tragi-Comedy of " The Witch." It may be remarked, that Eccles's music adheres more strictly to Sir W. D'Avenant's version than that attributed to Locke.

Folio. End of the XVIIth cent. [*Add. Mss.* 12,219.]

238.

A volume in the handwriting of John Immyns, the founder of the Madrigal Society, containing Madrigals and Motetts for

two, three, four, five, and six voices, by the following com-
posers : Josquin des Pres, Claude Le Jeune, Vaqueras,
Thomas Morley, Orlando di Lasso, Antonio Brumel,
William Byrd, Simone Molinaro, Thomas Weelkes, Andr.
Pevernage, Noe Faignient, Marc-Antonio Pordenoni, Fi-
lippo di Monte, Marc-Antonio Ingegneri, Paolo Masnelli,
Giovanni de Macque, Luca Marenzio, Benedetto Pallavicino,
John Bennett, Orazio Vecchi, Chrisostom Rubiconi, Leon
Leoni, Salomon Rossi, Girolamo Casati, Giov. Pier Luigi da
Palestrina, Jacques de Wert, Giov. Bernardo Colombi, Clan-
dio Monteverde, Marsilio Santini, Giovanni Croce, Gabriel
Fattorini, Annibal of Padua, Pomponio Nenna, Stefano Ro-
setto, and Agostino Agazzari.

For six voices.

Accend' i cor ˜.	J. de Wert	p. 161
Gratie oh' a poch'	S. Rosetto	. 285
Vagan per l'aria	A. Agazzari . . .	. 289
Ma lass' io.	id. . . .	. 293

Quarto.   Middle of the xviiith cent. [*Add. Mss.* 12,532.]

239.

" Chorus, by Mr. Wolfgang Mozart, 1765."

This composition for four voices, to the words " God is
our refuge," in the handwriting of Mozart when he was only
seven years of age, is attached to the printed copy of his
" Sonates pour le Clavecin, dediées à Madame la Comtesse
de Tessé, Œuvre 2. Paris," presented by his father to the
British Museum, in July, 1765. Obl. fol. Preserved in the
General Library of Printed Books.

OMISSIONS.

91*.

A volume containing Hymns and other pieces set to music,
adapted to the service of the Greek Church :

A Treatise on the signs used in Psalmody, with the ascending and descending
tones. Begin. ἀρχὴ · μέση · τίλος καὶ σύστημα. fol. 3.

Hymns called κικραγάρια, or exclamatory (from Ps. 141.), together with the
ἀναστάσιμοι, or verses to be sung on the Resurrection, etc., under the various tones. fol. 9.

The eleven ἰωθινα, or Matutinal Hymns, composed by the Emperor Leo, and
set to music by Johannes Glycæus. fol. 115 b.

See Fabricius, *Bibl. Græca*, vol. iii. p. 655. *edit.* Harles.

The Liturgy, or Mass of St. John Chrysostom. fol. 130 b.

Two Hymns ascribed to [Manuel] Chrysaphes. fol. 131 b.

The Liturgy of St. Basil (imperfect). fol. 133 b.

Small Quarto.   xvth cent. [*Harl. Mss.* 5544.]

123*.

A Treatise on Indian Music, in Persian, written in the year of
the Hegira, 1192. A.D. 1780. Octavo. [*Egerton Mss.* 793.]

INDEX.

The figures refer to the regular series of numbers in the Catalogue.

CORRECTIONS.

---

p. 3, *l.* 6. for *Ms. Sloane* read *Ms. Add.*

p. 7, *ll.* 24. 45. p. 22, *l.* 9. p. 62, *l.* 36. *for* e *read* è.

p. 15, *l.* 24. *for* vol. ii. *read* vol. i.

p. 17, *l.* 21. *for* Ste lo *read* Steso.

p. 19, *l.* 53. p. 21, *ll.* 57. 86. *for* è *read* e.

p. 20, *l.* 54. *for* tè (*as in the Ms.*) *read* te.

  ib. l. 85. *for* come le canta. (P. F. Tosi.) *read* come le canta P. F. Tosi.

p. 23, *l.* 25. *for* Egionto *read* E gionto.

  ib. l. 57. *for* sio *read* s'io.

  ib. l. 70. *for* xiith or xiiith cent. *we should, probably, substitute* xivth cent.

p. 27, *l.* 23. for *Sloane Ms.* read *Add. Ms.*

p. 46, *l.* 30. *for* plaudeus *read* plaudens.

p. 87, *l.* 7. *for* Phil. *read* Pierre.

G. Woodfall and Son, Printers, Angel Court, Skinner Street, London.

CPSIA information can be obtained
at www.ICGtesting.com
Printed in the USA
BVHW061454041218
534740BV00017B/550/P

9 780331 324297